Connecting
with Muslims

A GUIDE TO COMMUNICATING EFFECTIVELY

Fouad Masri

Foreword by Josh McDowell

IVP Books

An imprint of InterVarsity Press
Downers Grove, Illinois

InterVarsity Press
P.O. Box 1400, Downers Grove, IL 60515-1426
World Wide Web: www.ivpress.com
Email: email@ivpress.com

InterVarsity Press® is the book-publishing division of InterVarsity Christian Fellowship/USA®, a movement of students and faculty active on campus at hundreds of universities, colleges and schools of nursing in the United States of America, and a member movement of the International Fellowship of Evangelical Students. For information about local and regional activities, write Public Relations Dept., InterVarsity Christian Fellowship/USA, 6400 Schroeder Rd., P.O. Box 7895, Madison, WI 53707-7895, or visit the IVCF website at www.intervarsity.org.

All Scripture quotations, unless otherwise indicated, are taken from THE HOLY BIBLE, NEW INTERNATIONAL VERSION®, NIV® Copyright © 1973, 1978, 1984, 2011 by Biblica, Inc.™ Used by permission. All rights reserved worldwide.

While all stories in this book are true, some names and identifying information in this book have been changed to protect the privacy of the individuals involved.

Cover design: Cindy Kiple
Interior design: Beth Hagenberg
Images: tea set: Pam McLean/Getty Images
      coffee cup: malerapaso/Getty Images
      green tablecloth background: kyoshino/Getty Images
      flower border: © azat1976/iStockphoto

ISBN 978-0-8308-4420-3 (print)
ISBN 978-0-8308-9590-8 (digital)

Printed in the United States of America ♾

Library of Congress Cataloging-in-Publication Data
Masri, Fouad.
  Connecting with Muslims : a guide to communicating effectively / Fouad
Masri.
     pages cm
  Includes bibliographical references.
  ISBN 978-0-8308-4420-3 (pbk. : alk. paper)
  1. Missions to Muslims. 2. Jesus Christ—Islamic interpretations. 3.
Christianity and other religions—Islam. 4.
Islam—Relations—Christianity. I. Title.
  BV2625.M35 2014
  266.0088'297—dc23
                                                            2014005168

| P | 18 | 17 | 16 | 15 | 14 | 13 | 12 | 11 | 10 | 9 | 8 | 7 | 6 | 5 | 4 | 3 | 2 |
| Y | 29 | 28 | 27 | 26 | 25 | 24 | 23 | 22 | 21 | 20 | 19 | 18 | 17 | 16 | 15 |

To my precious family,

whose love and prayers have

helped me finish this book

Contents

Foreword

Christians have not always been very aware of our Muslim neighbors. We may not have thought much about the quiet shopkeeper checking out our order or the young graduate student at the library in her hijab. But after 9/11, Christians became alert to Muslims, and we didn't always respond well. Many saw all Muslims as threats to be feared. Some even felt compelled to strike back and hurt those who hurt us. However, this is not the heart of Jesus our Messiah!

Other Christians soon turned this around and opened their eyes to the new opportunities for evangelism and outreach. Muslims are not the enemy—they are people created in the image of God, priceless in God's sight. Jesus lived for them and died for them, and Christians likewise ought to love them and share the good news of the gospel with them.

But this hasn't always gone well either. Sometimes Christians have been so intent on winning converts that they have tried to argue Muslims into the kingdom, debating about theology or mixing up religion with politics. Some of our Muslim neighbors have been on the receiving end of sales pitches that brushed aside their faith and tried to sell them a Jesus that didn't make any sense to them. We have tried to get them into our churches without first welcoming them into our hearts and homes. This is not the way of Jesus.

That's why I'm grateful for Fouad Masri's *Connecting with Muslims*. This book shows how Christians and Muslims can connect with one another in real relationships of respect and trust. Masri is an Arab Christian and a skilled communicator who can explain the cultural differences and bridge the gap between different worlds. He explains where Muslims are coming from in ways that Christians can understand, and he explains Christianity in ways that make sense to Muslims.

Make no mistake: Masri is clear about the differences between Christianity and Islam, and this book will help the reader answer the tough questions about what we believe and what is really true. But he does so winsomely, out of shared relationship and community. Connecting and communicating go hand in hand. When trust is built, truth can be heard. Then we will not be "us" over here and "them" over there, but a community of friends who can all journey toward God together.

So I hope this book will help you understand how to connect with Muslims, but more importantly, I hope that you will actually live it out. Invite that shopkeeper for a cup of tea. Welcome that graduate student into your home. Get to know them not just as "Muslims," but as Khalid and Sorayah, or Abdul and Minya, friends and neighbors, beloved by yourself and by God.

Josh McDowell

Introduction

The Communication Gap

—●—

WITH RECENT LEAPS AND BOUNDS in technology and travel, the planet is no doubt getting smaller. And yet, how well can we say we understand Muslims? And how well do Muslims understand Christians?

There are obvious gaps when it comes to Christian and Muslim relationships. Christians don't really understand Islam, and Muslims don't really understand Christianity. The divide between Christians and Muslims is at once social, spiritual and personal. In particular, two major gaps in communication and accessibility are impeding Christians' communication with Muslims.

The first gap is a lack of understanding on the Christian's part to Muslims and the religion of Islam. The second is a lack of communication tools that would help the Christian to effectively share the gospel of Christ.

An English teacher in Afghanistan (a Muslim country) was asked by a student, "Why are you a Christian?" The teacher stared at the student and avoided the question. When asked why she did so, her answer was, "I do not know Islam or what they believe about Christians."

An evangelist was asked by a Sunni Muslim civil engineer,

"What does the Bible say about Muhammad?" The evangelist read from John 10 and claimed that the Bible calls Muhammad a thief and a murderer. That was the last conversation the evangelist had with this engineer.

Unfortunately, Christians' communication with Muslims has been overwhelmingly insensitive, and at times downright offensive. Communication with Muslims is characterized by an argumentative spirit and heated discussion. Instead of focusing on productive dialogue, too many believers are aggressive and uncompromising in their approach and end up alienating Muslims rather than befriending them. Discussions between Christians and Muslims that at first looked promising frequently dissolve into an impasse instead of resulting in an open pathway to understanding. On the whole, Christians are not finding accessible ways to connect with Muslims.

My hope is that this book will encourage and provide believers with communication and relationship tools to bridge the communication gap with Muslims. I hope that as you read these chapters you feel empowered to show love to Muslims as God brings them into your path.

My goal is to see believers have a crystal-clear biblical understanding of Islam and a variety of ministry tools for effective communications with Muslims. This book will introduce simple, conversational tools that cut to the core issues of Islam without offending Muslims or sidestepping the truth.

Cross the Street

You don't have to listen too closely at church to hear people sharing about what short-term mission trips they are going on. It even sounds fancy to say, "I'm going to Beirut," or "I'm going to Indonesia" or "I'm going to Morocco." Many Western believers have taken the plunge to cross the ocean to minister to

Muslims. Don't get me wrong—these overseas trips are replete with amazing opportunities to meet new people and to engage with Muslims and explore a new culture. Even I go on them frequently. But in reality, there are Muslims living just across the street who have never been ministered to by their own neighbors.

Many Muslims have never been invited inside an American home, and many have never been visited by an American. Even more Muslims have never been invited to a Christian home and have never been visited by a Christian. *Christianity Today* reports that 42.5 percent of Muslims in North America do not personally know any Christians![1]

A young lady recently took the Bridges: Christians Connecting with Muslims course (www.bridgesstudy.com) that is offered by the Crescent Project (www.crescentproject.org), a series that trains Christians how to communicate with Muslims in an effective and respectful way. This young lady discovered that she had a classmate from Egypt, and she decided to visit her classmate's family in their home. As they chatted over Egyptian tea, talking about the beauty of Egypt, her classmate's mother looked over her teacup and said, "You are a nice American."

Slightly surprised, the young lady replied, "Thank you."

The mother continued, "We've lived in this house for six years. You are the first American to visit us." In *six* years, she was the *first* American to visit!

Who will welcome Muslims? Who will invite them into their homes for coffee or a meal? Will it take all of us six years or more before we have a strong enough relationship with Muslims to be invited into their homes? Why don't we invite them to our house? Let them see our religion. Let them see our faith. Romans 12:13 exhorts us, "Share with the Lord's people who are in need. Practice hospitality." What greater need do Muslims have than to know who the Savior is? Learning to practice hospitality—a

practice that is so natural and has such deep roots in the Middle
East—can be our "in" to minister to Muslims

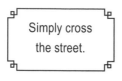
Simply cross
the street.

from the comfort of our own homes. It isn't
necessary to cross an ocean. You can simply
cross the street.

Intentional Engagement: Your Role in the Great Commission

Two thousand years ago, Christ asked us to engage with others
and to be intentional about witnessing to others. But now an
incredibly apparent gap exists between Christians and Muslims.
Christians are still called *kafirs* ("unbelievers") by many Muslims
today. Conflict, wars and misunderstanding prevail where connection, rapport and a free exchange of ideas are needed.

Many Christians still subscribe to several myths about
Muslims. First is the sentiment among many Western Christians
that Muslims hate us. But so many amazing opportunities await
us when we commit to meeting Muslims and talking to them
about Jesus. Too often, fear prevents believers from taking the
initiative to get to know Muslims, or even engaging in light conversation with them. I have to ask: what's so frightening about
talking to Muslims?

A second myth is that Muslims are not interested in Jesus or
Christianity. A third and even more upsetting myth is that God
himself doesn't care about Muslims and Islam. But it is clear that
from the beginning God cared for *all* races and *all* religions. It is
time to bridge the gap that we have created between us.

In the Middle East, I saw the casualties of raw hatred. I
watched Christians build walls of fear so high they forgot the key
word of the Great Commission in Matthew 28: "Go." Regret-
tably, this same tragedy occurs today among Christians who,
overcome with fear, view Muslims as the enemy.

Are Muslims not worthy of the gospel message? Can everyday Christians begin seeing Muslims through Jesus' eyes? Are there ways to bridge the gospel to the Muslim mind and heart? Walls can fall down when even one Christian infused with the love of Christ becomes an active ambassador to Muslims.

The journey starts when one Christian decides to meet Muslims where they are: across the street, next door, in the supermarket checkout line, at the mall, on the running trail, at the gas station. Where you are, Muslims are there too. Right now is the time to start capitalizing on the smallest of opportunities to intentionally engage with Muslims, to begin conversations with them as you would conversations with anyone else. It happens over a cup of coffee, or with an invitation to a meal, or with a smile and a compliment at the cash register. *Now* is the time to begin inviting Muslims into our homes and lives so that they, too, may have the same hope and assurance that we Christians have.

THE PURPOSE OF THIS BOOK: HOW TO COMMUNICATE EFFECTIVELY

We can't ignore Muslims anymore. While millions of followers of Islam are becoming our neighbors in North America and Europe, Christians feel confused and helpless about Islam and about how to effectively communicate with Muslims. A telling survey conducted in 2002 by the Ethics and Public Policy Center and Beliefnet discovered that 77 percent of evangelicals have an unfavorable view of Islam, and yet 97 percent deem it "very important" or "somewhat important" to evangelize US Muslims![2] With this conflicting attitude, what will serve as the catalyst for evangelization? A fresh perspective is needed in order to see Muslims through the eyes of Jesus instead of the eyes of CNN.

Many books published since 9/11 tend to fall into two ex-
tremes: they either trash Islam or sugarcoat it. Some books help
Christians grasp the basics of Islam but lack action steps to
impact the Muslim community in culturally appropriate, Christ-
centered ways. Such texts leave the reader with head knowledge
about Islam but without insight into Muslims or practical ways
to reach them.

It takes more than a guilt-laden sermon to come to the real-
ization, "Perhaps I could share the gospel with a Muslim." *It
takes seeing Muslims as Jesus sees them.* We know not *all* Muslims
are terrorists, but we question, aren't they just as diametrically
opposed to Jesus? We must start thinking about how a Christian
would seek to befriend anyone so seemingly hostile to the basic
tenets of Christianity. We must start thinking about how God
could use us to impart the gospel to someone so set in his ways.

I am sure you agree on the need to go, but some important
questions to ask may include the following: How can I communicate in a way that Muslims understand? How can I begin a
conversation? How do I end the conversation? How do I build
a relationship of trust with Muslims I meet? Are there words or
ideas that can help me be effective in my communication? Do I
have to be an expert in theology and debating strategies in order
to befriend a Muslim?

Feelings of fear toward Muslims must be replaced with compassion and love based on Christ's command. Feelings of in-
adequacy must be replaced with courage based on the presence
of the Holy Spirit in our lives. Feelings of hesitancy must be
replaced with initiative and action as we use effective communication tools.

I wrote this book to equip you with the tools to understand
and respond to Muslim neighbors, coworkers or acquaintances
in a way that is biblical and Christ-centered. This book seeks to

share testimonies and methods that will take the pressure off and instead fill you with hope and expectation for your next encounter with a Muslim.

You do not need a PhD in Islam to share your faith with a Muslim. Instead, you need to know Christ, have a heart of an ambassador and an array of effective communication tools. This book focuses on practical ways to initiate conversations with Muslims (part 1) and addresses seven critical questions that Muslims ask about Jesus and the Christian faith (part 2). This book provides readers with insights into Muslim culture so that believers can remain sensitive to how Muslims might react to certain ideas and approaches. After learning the "bridges" between Islam and Christianity and growing confident from reading the real-life stories of those who have engaged with Muslims, readers will be better equipped to winsomely initiate conversations that guide Muslims to Jesus, without arguing or awkward debating! My hope is to help you move beyond fear and skepticism and jump into *action*. I pray that this book will help you connect with Muslims and share the gospel with them effectively.

Have a heart of an ambassador.

Part One

Practical Ways to
Connect with Muslims

Chapter 1

Our Role in the Great Commission

—◆—

URGED TO LOVE, URGED TO PRAY

Where I grew up, a civil war gripped the country. I was born and raised in Beirut, Lebanon, which is a small country in the Middle East about the size of Connecticut. While the country is beautiful, the lengthy civil war was completely ugly. It created in me a hatred for foreigners and fellow countrymen. In my mind, I placed them in either a religious or political box. To me, individuals were no longer just individuals—they were defined as either friends or foes.

During the war, I routinely witnessed Israeli jets flying over Beirut on reconnaissance missions. The planes roaring overhead would break the sound barrier and bomb both the capital city and the mountainous areas. These ringing sounds in my ears only reminded me of the Arab-Israeli war and of family members on my mom's side who fought in the Golan Heights. Seeing and hearing the Israeli jets and bombs fostered in me a deep-seated hatred of the Jewish people.

Not only was I nursing my loathing of the Israelis, but I was also harboring acute disgust of the Palestinians because a friend from high school was killed by them. Waleed, my close friend and soccer teammate, was taking a walk on a Saturday morning at 9 o'clock, smoking a cigarette. Shelling from the Palestinian Liberation Organization (PLO) militia killed him. I hated the Palestinians for killing my friend.

I grew up with this abhorrence during the Lebanese War, hating Jewish people and hating Palestinians. I believed both people groups ought to go away. I knew my hatred didn't reflect the heart of Jesus, but I just wanted the war to be finished.

Amazingly, it was the war that prompted me to start studying different religions and prompted me to look more closely at the teachings of Jesus. The Christian faith had come to my family when my grandfather was saved in Toledo, Ohio, in 1914. He returned to Lebanon and brought the gospel back to his family. As I, years later after my grandfather was saved, revisited the teachings of Christ, I discovered that weapons don't kill people; people kill people. Even a cursory review of history shows that humans have filled their hearts with hate. Humans have filled their hearts with anger and sin. It is the hardness of humans' hearts that results in humans' killing one another. The atomic bomb, the hydrogen bomb, the neutron bomb: we are ever more creative in how we utterly destroy human life. Still, the root problem remains: sin.

As I continued to study the teachings of Jesus, I was especially struck by the story of how Christ washed the feet of his disciples. I was really shocked that Jesus would even wash the feet of Judas Iscariot, fully knowing Judas would betray him. It was a humbling moment for me as I read, and I knew that Jesus was the Messiah. I knew that Jesus was the Savior. I knew that Jesus' teachings were correct, but at the time, for me, it was all head knowledge. I wrestled with how I could submit my will and my life to Jesus, especially in the middle of my country's chaos. A terrible tragedy spurred me to action.

A family friend was eating dinner with his wife and four children. His youngest child was two years old and had spilled his milk at dinner. This friend picked up his son to take him to the bathroom to wash up, and a mortar shell blasted through the balcony door and exploded in the middle of the table. Our friend made his way back to the kitchen and found his wife and three other children in pieces. With a plastic bag and a heavy heart, he picked up the remnants of his family and buried them.

That was my trigger to move my head knowledge of the unique love of Jesus to my heart. I was finally ready to fully commit my life to Christ. I went to my room, closed the door behind me and knelt by my bed. I prayed to the Lord, "Lord Jesus, when you came to earth, you healed the sick. You raised the dead. You washed the feet of your disciples. The more hate there is in Lebanon, the more I want to be a soldier of love. The more war there is in Lebanon, the more I want to be a soldier of peace. Forgive me for my sin. Forgive me for hating Palestinians and Israelis. Change my heart and make me a new person. I want to follow you as my Savior and Lord."

It was a life-changing moment for me. I started to pray for the Jewish people. I started to pray for the Palestinians. When you are a follower of Jesus, when you are committed to the teachings of Christ, when you have received Jesus as your Savior, you don't see people by their religion, race or background. You don't see people by their level of education. You see them as God's

> When you are a follower of Jesus, when you are committed to the teachings of Christ, when you have received Jesus as your Savior, you don't see people by their religion, race or background. You don't see people by their level of education. You see them as God's creation. You see they need a Savior. Like you and I need a Savior, they also need a Savior.

creation. You see they need a Savior. Like you and I need a Savior, they also need a Savior.

COMMANDED BY JESUS

Just as I needed Jesus, millions of others are in need of Jesus, including millions of Muslims. As followers of Christ, we enjoy forgiveness, the community of God's family and hope of eternal joy. On the other side, in a place of misunderstanding and misinformation, our Muslim friends are walking in a spiritual Sahara, plagued by guilt, uncertainty and fear.

Action Point

Pray for Muslims regularly. Pray that God would open up constructive conversations with them about Jesus.

As ambassadors for Jesus, our goal is to construct a bridge by which our friends can cross over from misunderstanding to truth, from fear to faith. However, paralyzed with fear, many Christians hesitate to reach out to Muslims to offer them the same hope and security Jesus offered to them. But let us consider the question, "Is engaging with Muslims really that scary?"

In Matthew 28:18, Jesus says, "All authority in heaven and on earth has been given to me." Who has all the authority? Jesus does. Having just defeated death itself, he prepared to ascend to his rightful throne, and he claimed to hold all power in heaven and on earth.

Jesus continues, "Therefore go and make disciples of all nations, baptizing them in the name of the Father and of the Son and of the Holy Spirit, and teaching them to obey

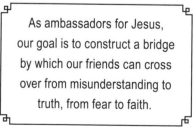

As ambassadors for Jesus, our goal is to construct a bridge by which our friends can cross over from misunderstanding to truth, from fear to faith.

everything I have commanded you. And surely I am with you always, to the very end of the age" (Matthew 28:19-20). What does Jesus say to do? *"Go."* Reach out. Take the initiative. Share the good news of the gospel with those who are in need.

Ignoring the command of Jesus to "go and make disciples of all nations" is not an option. Who will welcome the Muslim family who just moved into the area? Who will befriend the Muslim neighbor down the street? Who will reach out to the Muslims sitting at the coffee shop? As the hands and feet of Jesus, *we* must welcome them. We must take care of them, regardless if they become Christians or not.

We need not fear Muslims or reaching out to Muslims because Jesus' mandate to us is fully funded. When you are sent out by Jesus, you are not going in your own name. You are going in the name above all names. Under his authority, in his power, you *must* take initiative—you *must* go.

I have been serving at Crescent Project since its founding in 1993. Crescent Project is a Christian organization that exists to share the hope of Christ with Muslims. At Crescent Project, we long to see a day when fear is replaced with love and millions of Christians are actively sharing the truth of Christ with millions of Muslims for the glory of God.

A friend of mine once told me, "Fouad, you need to close Crescent Project."

I asked, "Why?"

He claimed, "God can save Muslims without your help."

Of course he can. But two thousand years ago, Jesus commanded his disciples to

> We need not fear Muslims or reaching out to Muslims because Jesus' mandate to us is fully funded. When you are sent out by Jesus, you are not going in your own name. You are going in the name above all names. Under his authority, in his power, you *must* take initiative—you *must* go.

go, and as disciples of Christ, we, too, are called to go. God has chosen that the gospel message will go out through his people.

Jesus' disciples were not the most powerful or influential people. Many had weaknesses and challenges that could hinder them from impacting their generation. However, Christ commanded them and used them to proclaim his teachings across the known world. Likewise, our challenges and weaknesses do not negate the need to implement the Lord's command in our own lives. When we are weak, God is strong. When we depend on God, he will transform our weaknesses and make us strong.

Jesus still commands us to get involved and share the good news. Jesus expects us to take the initiative, but we do it in his power, not our own. "Going" has nothing to do with my own ability. Going is not an act to be feared. When I go, I am under the name and authority and ability of Christ. My only role is to go and invite people into relationship, into friendship, and to share the gospel with them.

Bridging the gap with Muslims is part of our role on earth. John was sent to testify to, and witness, the coming of Jesus (John 1:8). We know it is impossible to form deep friendships with every Muslim on earth, and so we must focus on testifying and witnessing to those we do encounter. Being a witness is about proclaiming the good news to others. To witness is to give an account of the story of the Messiah. It is to share your story of how you became a follower of Jesus. When we witness to Muslims, we give an account of the salvation that Jesus offers them and an account of our faith and our hope. Jesus didn't just walk on earth. He intentionally witnessed to others. This book will prepare you with the tools to bridge the gap in communication with Muslims so that your witness to them will become even more effective.

MAKE AN OFFER

I was driving from Columbus, Ohio, to Indianapolis, Indiana, one evening. It was raining cats and dogs, so I stopped at a gas station for a few minutes to take a break. Another car pulled up, and three young men exited. The first man, a Palestinian, had on a white cap (*taqiyah*) and had a beard without a mustache, a sign that he was with the Muslim Brotherhood, a rather conservative Islamic organization. The second man was a tall Yemeni. The third man was Eritrean, and he began to pump gas in their car.

I made a beeline for the first man, since he was acting as the leader of the group. I greeted him, "*As-salaamu alaikum,*" a welcoming phrase typically used to greet Muslims, meaning "peace be upon you." He responded in kind, "*Wa alaikum asalaam,*" which means, "and upon you be peace." I introduced myself to him and told him that I had a gift for him. I returned to my car to retrieve a copy of the *Injeel,* the Arabic word for the New Testament.

Offering him the text, I said to him, "My friend, I want to give you the Injeel, the message of God. God keeps it to enlighten us." Taking the gift, he replied, "Oh, we Muslims love Prophet Jesus." Having finished pumping gas, the Eritrean man came over to us and took the Injeel from his friend's hand. He said, "What? The Injeel?" and started to read it in Arabic with a mimicking voice, making fun of it. As he began to read John 1 aloud, "In the beginning was the Word, and the Word was with God, and the Word was God," he trailed off and began to read the Word silently. Soon he looked up and asked me, "Can I keep this book?"

His Palestinian friend objected, saying, "No, this is my book." I stopped them and said, "It's not a problem. I have another Injeel." The Yemeni protested, "You are giving my friends an Injeel. What about me? I want an Injeel." That day, I gave three copies of the Injeel to those young students.

In response to this story, some people have responded, "Well, they didn't become Christians." What they don't realize is that my job—your job—is not to make anyone anything! I'm not asking them to change their religion. I'm not asking them to stop eating hummus. I'm not asking them to dress any differently. I'm simply asking them to read the words of Jesus. That's it. We are trusting God to use the message of the gospel to change their minds and hearts.

Action Point

Gift giving solidifies friendship in Middle Eastern culture. Be prepared with a gift to offer Muslim friends, something spiritual in nature that focuses on the teachings of Jesus.

My role in the Great Commission is not to ensure that Muslims say yes to the gospel. My responsibility is to take the initiative and be an ambassador to Muslims by showing them respect, love, friendship and compassion. My responsibility is to share the gospel of Jesus with them. God will move in the hearts and minds of Muslims. God promises that his Word will never return void (Isaiah 55:11). As ambassadors for Christ, *we* do not make people citizens of God's kingdom. God himself is the one who makes someone a citizen of heaven. Our job is to clearly explain the gospel and leave the results to God.

As ambassadors of the kingdom of God, we invite people to visit the kingdom—to hear the teachings of the kingdom and reflect on the values of the kingdom. We cannot make anyone a citizen of the kingdom. We can only represent it, in word and deed.

> As ambassadors for Christ, *we* do not make people citizens of God's kingdom. God himself is the one who makes someone a citizen of heaven. Our job is to clearly explain the gospel and leave the results to God.

A THEOLOGY OF MISSIONS

The book of Isaiah helps frame what "missions" looks like in a local context. The command to "go" in Matthew 28 can be seen as an extension of Isaiah 6, in which Isaiah responds to God's call to participate in his Great Commission to bring others to himself.

In the year that King Uzziah died, I saw the Lord, high and exalted, seated on a throne; and the train of his robe filled the temple. Above him were seraphim, each with six wings: With two wings they covered their faces, with two they covered their feet, and with two they were flying. And they were calling to one another:

"Holy, holy, holy is the LORD Almighty;
the whole earth is full of his glory."

At the sound of their voices the doorposts and thresholds shook and the temple was filled with smoke.

"Woe to me!" I cried. "I am ruined! For I am a man of unclean lips, and I live among a people of unclean lips, and my eyes have seen the King, the LORD Almighty."

Then one of the seraphim flew to me with a live coal in his hand, which he had taken with tongs from the altar. With it he touched my mouth and said, "See, this has touched your lips; your guilt is taken away and your sin atoned for."

Then I heard the voice of the Lord saying, "Whom shall I send? And who will go for us?"

And I said, "Here am I. Send me!" (Isaiah 6:1-8)

The Lord was looking for someone to *go* and invest their time, talents and treasures in the work he had planned. Isaiah was eager to be sent by God as an ambassador of the Lord. He didn't shy away from what God had designed. Instead, Isaiah piped up immediately and submitted his will to the Lord. He didn't know what the plan was; he just decided he had to be a part of it.

Action Point

Ask God to send *you*. Trust that he will open up opportunities for you to reach out to Muslims.

A theology of missions involves submitting oneself to God, determining to participate in the work that the Lord has purposed by "going" to others, all the while trusting that God will bring about the changes in people's hearts and lives. In this sense, we are all Isaiahs, called by the Lord to be sent to those who do not know him, whether near or far. The mission field is right here, right now, right next door.

If there is a college campus near your church, you live on a mission field. If you have a neighbor, you live on a mission field. If there is a mosque within driving distance, you live on a mission field. If Muslims live in your

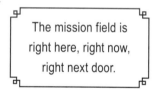

The mission field is right here, right now, right next door.

Action Point

Visit a local college campus and do a prayer walk around the grounds. Pray for the Muslims on campus, that they would be reached with the gospel by fellow students. If the opportunity arises, meet a Muslim student and open up a friendly conversation.

community—and make no mistake; they do—then you live on a mission field. These mission fields may mystify you or even frighten you. Perhaps you will be tempted to look the other way, seeking an easier group of people to reach. But trust me: the field is ready for harvest, if only you and your church will embrace the challenge and respond to the need.

> The field is ready for harvest, if only you and your church will embrace the challenge and respond to the need.

Matthew 9:35-38 reads,

Jesus went through all the towns and villages, teaching in their synagogues, proclaiming the good news of the kingdom and healing every disease and sickness. When he saw the crowds, he had compassion on them, because they were harassed and helpless, like sheep without a shepherd. Then he said to his disciples, "The harvest is plentiful but the workers are few. Ask the Lord of the harvest, therefore, to send out workers into his harvest field."

Jesus was a Jewish carpenter; he had a business to tend to. Jesus himself chose to *go*—to share the good news of the kingdom that he is the Messiah, that he is the Savior, that people can know that the prophecies have been fulfilled, that they can have salvation and join Jesus in the greatest wedding festival and the greatest feast in the kingdom of God. He followed his own command to go. Will you go too?

God's plan is for all of us to deliver his message. Replace fear with courage and take the initiative to talk to a Muslim.

Hope Worth Sharing

The salvation that Christ offers is the only hope for all. It is imperative that the hope of Jesus Christ is known. Astoundingly, God has chosen us—broken, weak, sinful, but *redeemed* people—to be a part of his plan to bring all peoples

Action Point

Instead of following your regular schedule, make a date to visit a local Middle Eastern restaurant or a coffee shop where you've seen Muslims before and strike up a conversation with one. It could turn into a meaningful friendship.

to himself. God desires that everyone share in the redemption he purchased through the sacrifice of his Son, and he has called us to bring his living water to the desert. John 15:16 says, "You did not choose me, but I chose you and appointed you so that you might go and bear fruit—fruit that will last." We must not be selfish with the good news, hoarding the grace that saved us. We must not be selfish with the gospel.

> We must not be selfish with the good news, hoarding the grace that saved us. We must not be selfish with the gospel.

In Houston, Texas, I met up with a high school friend. He mentioned that his wife was studying to be a lawyer and that she would meet us after her class. While my friend and I were catching up, his wife joined us. My friend introduced me, mentioning that I am an evangelical minister. Shockingly, she responded, "You evangelicals make me sick."

I said to her, "Nice to meet you too." As we sat down again, I remarked, "I hope we evangelicals don't offend you."

She responded, "No, you don't offend me, but Jesus is not for everybody. Jesus is for the Christians only." I laughed to myself because Jesus was a Jewish carpenter; there were no Christians in those days.

Over our meal I asked her, "I understand you're a lawyer?" When she said that she was, I asked her if she had heard of AIDS. She said she had, so I continued, "What if Congress decided to offer a grant to an American scientist, and that American scientist discovered the cure for AIDS? Wouldn't that be great?"

She said, "Well, sure, that would be remarkable. Such a discovery would solve a lot of problems and save a lot of lives."

I persisted, "What if, after the cure for AIDS were discovered, Congress decided that since the cure was made by an American and funded by America, only US citizens would be allowed the cure?"

She vehemently replied, "No, they cannot do that."

I rejoined, "Why not? It's our money. It's our discovery."

After a moment of contemplation, she responded, "Well, there is a moral obligation to offer the cure to everyone who needs it."

I countered, "A moral obligation? What morality are you talking about? The morality of power, that the one who has the might decides?"

Confused, she asked, "What do you mean?"

I said to her, "The morality you are talking about is the morality of Jesus. Jesus said that he gave to us freely, and so we are to give to others freely. What we received freely we must share freely. We Christians are not trying to offend anybody. We have found the cure for sin. We are sinners who have found the Savior. We just want to share him. People don't have to follow, but we have to share him out of a moral obligation."

More than ever, people today need to hear that Jesus loves them, regardless of their response, regardless of their situation. We are the hands and feet of Jesus, and we must get the message out.

GOD IS OUR COACH

As believers in Jesus, we believe in the Great Commission, which Jesus gave to his disciples, to reach all nations. It is Christ who leads us as we reach Muslims around the world. Our job is not to make the Muslim a Christian. Our job is to show Muslims the love of Christ.

When I first came to America as an international student, I was intrigued by American football. Over Christmas break, I asked my roommate Amos to explain the game to me. He started, "Eleven players play from each team."

Our job is not to make the Muslim a Christian. Our job is to show Muslims the love of Christ.

I exclaimed, "What?! Only eleven? It must be a high-injury game. There are so many replacements on the sidelines."

He clarified, "No, no. There's offense, defense, kicking teams and special teams."

I nodded. "Okay, great. So when does a player know it's his turn?"

He responded, "The coach will tell them."

Our coach is the Messiah from Nazareth. On his team, we all play, regardless of age, education or ability. We are all on the team. Too often in my life I stood on the sidelines with the Lord telling me, "Fouad, get in the game." And too often I told him, "Lord, that's offense. I play defense." It is time for us to be in the game, giving 100 percent of ourselves to the cause.

Action Point

Invite a Muslim friend to dinner or coffee at your home, or visit a Muslim at his or her home. Make an effort to meet Muslims.

Maybe the Lord has put a Muslim friend on your heart whom he wants you to call. Maybe you know a Muslim who has questions about Jesus. Or perhaps you are being prompted to invite a Muslim to your home for dinner. Or possibly God is calling you to go overseas to reach out to Muslims. Regardless of our personal calling from the Lord, let's get involved in the game of life to share the hope we have in Jesus with others.

Do not forfeit your God-given role as an ambassador for Christ!

Closing Prayer: *Our heavenly Father, thank you for sending Jesus to be the Savior of all humanity. Thank you that I am called a friend of Jesus and an ambassador for Christ. Thank you for my role in the Great Commission. Fill me with your Holy Spirit and empower me to be a witness of what you have done in my life. In Christ's name, amen.*

Chapter 2

Compelling Evangelism

Witnessing Like Jesus

—◆—

Compelling Conversation

In discussing ministry to Muslims, we use the word *compelling* because we want them to talk to us more. The intention of dialoguing with Muslims is to have thoughtful, meaningful conversations—not to enter a boxing match of theology and philosophy.

The Bible records that our Messiah lived and ministered on earth. Christ was born in the city of Bethlehem, raised in the city of Nazareth and went from town to town proclaiming the good news. The Messiah Jesus ministered in cities and towns throughout Samaria, Judea and Galilee. The life of Christ is full of conversations in which the listeners were compelled to seek to know more and to commit to a change of direction by following the Messiah.

Jesus lived a lifestyle of evangelism. Wherever he went, his actions, miracles and conversations compelled listeners to learn more about the kingdom of God and the message of salvation. Evangelism comes from the Greek word *euangelion*, which means "good news." Evangelism is simply sharing the good news, not necessarily creating converts.

The angel told the shepherds, "Do not be afraid. I bring you good news that will cause great joy for all the people. Today in the town of David a Savior has been born to you; he is the Messiah, the Lord" (Luke 2:10-11). The good news we are sharing is the same news the angel shared, and the same news Jesus later shared: that Jesus is the Savior of the world.

For successful ministry among Muslims, we need to live out a lifestyle that follows the lifestyle of our Messiah. We must seize opportunities to generate compelling conversations that lead our friends to a point of decision.

THE MESSAGE, NOT THE RESULTS

When I was studying at Fuller Theological Seminary, one of my classmates once discouraged me from searching out ministry opportunities with Muslims. He dissuaded me, "You have to work where God is working."

I questioned him, "What does that mean, to work where God is working?"

He explained, "You have to put your money and people where there is fruit. Maybe in Africa, or Asia or Latin America. But Muslims . . . I don't know, Fouad. How many Muslims have you seen come to Christ? One, two?"

I started to think he was right, that maybe I should "surf the wave of missions," go into a "fruitful" ministry. But then the Lord spoke to me again. He pointed out to me how he was working when Jesus hung on that cross. How many converts and followers did Jesus have? Three. One: the thief, who received him as Savior. Two: Mary. Three: John, the disciple. Even on that terrible day, God was working to save souls.

> How many people did I talk to about Christ? To how many people did I offer resources and materials? How many people did I represent Christ to?

The struggle we have today is that the "results" we see and the numbers we count are *not* the proof that there is ministry going on. And if we're honest with ourselves, what are the results we are looking for? The results are not converts. No, the results are about how many people we reach. How many people did I talk to about Christ? To how many people did I offer resources and materials? How many people did I represent Christ to? We need to focus on the whole picture.

Action Point

Think about setting a goal about how many Muslims you want to meet each week or each month. Set a goal that is realistic and attainable. Then act! Extend that invitation to coffee or to a dinner at your home. Set goals for how many copies of the Injeel you want to gift to your new Muslim friends. Be intentional about engaging with Muslims.

THE ART OF EVANGELISM

A few years back, *Time* magazine boasted a provocative cover story: "Should Christians Convert Muslims?"[1] In my opinion, this was an inappropriate title. How would Muslims feel if I were to put out such a story titled "Should Muslims Kill Christians?" I fully believe that *we* do not convert anybody. We are ambassadors!

Similarly, I am often asked if I'm a missionary. Typically I respond in turn, "What's a missionary?" Many people say that a missionary is someone who makes people Christians. When I hear such a response, I must reply, "Then no, I'm not a missionary. I don't make anyone a Christian. God does."

We don't convert anyone. We want to love people and share with them about our faith. We're encouraging Christians to read the Qur'an. We're asking Muslims to read the Bible. We are asking Christians and Muslims to *connect*.

Our Lord and Savior mastered the art of evangelism. As his disciples, we also must master the art of evangelism. It is the art of sharing the good news. As Christ's ambassadors, we are to learn, grow and excel in the art of sharing the message of forgiveness.

The art of "not evangelism" is not biblical. The Bible exhorts us to share the good news of Christ in season and out of season. "Preach the word; be prepared in season and out of season; correct, rebuke and encourage—with great patience and careful instruction" (2 Timothy 4:2). This verse applies to us! We must always be ready to share about the hope within us, regardless if it is a convenient time for us or not. So long as our friend is seeking the Messiah, we need to be prepared to share.

It is crucial that we know our message. What are we sharing? Who are we talking about? What *is* the good news? We need to know the art of evangelism. What are we inviting people to do?

ARE YOU READY FOR AN OPEN DOOR?

In John 7:37-38, Jesus proclaims that he is the living water: "Let anyone who is thirsty come to me and drink. Whoever believes in me, as Scripture has said, rivers of living water will flow from within them." As believers, we have experienced how Jesus has quenched our thirst. Muslims, too, desperately need this source of living water.

This is our message: Jesus is the living water! In reaching out to Muslims, we invite them to share in the gospel, to know the one who is the living water they seek. It is time we pray that the Lord would open doors for authentic ministry to Muslims. I trust that when we pray, "Lord, I am ready to share about you. Please open the door!" that God will open doors for us. But I must caution you not to pray this prayer unless you are ready for those doors to be opened. In turn, we must be open to using the opportunities the Lord provides for us.

OPENING THE DOOR

In his ministry, Jesus was entirely strategic about his approach. There are many passages in the Bible in which to study how Jesus effectively communicated the good news of salvation. The story of Jesus and the Samaritan woman in John 4 is an excellent model to master the art of evangelism. It is one that sheds light on how the Lord purposefully moved what could have been a superficial exchange into deeper waters.

Action Point

Remind yourself that you may be the only Christian that a Muslim speaks with today. Offer your time to them by opening a conversation, no matter how small. God is working at all times. Take the initiative!

In the next few pages, I would like to visit this passage more closely and glean from it lessons for sharing the gospel. Let us walk through this chapter and draw out key elements that will empower us as we connect with Muslims.

Begin on a tangible level: The physical level. "So he came to a town in Samaria called Sychar, near the plot of ground Jacob had given to his son Joseph. Jacob's well was there, and Jesus, tired as he was from the journey, sat down by the well. It was about noon. When a Samaritan woman came to draw water, Jesus said to her, 'Will you give me a drink?' (His disciples had gone into the town to buy food.)" (John 4:5-8).

On his way back to Galilee from Judea, the text says that Jesus "had to go through Samaria" (John 4:4). In fact, this is not the case. He did not "have" to go through Samaria, as there were other routes he could have taken, although the fastest route was through Samaria. Many Jews avoided communing and interacting with Samaritans by going around Samaria. But Christ had a different strategy; he went *through* Samaria. In ministry to

Muslims, some of you will go "through" a country or will move "through" your community. The willingness to go out of your way to interact with people who might otherwise not encounter another believer that day is a key strategy element.

> The willingness to go out of your way to interact with people who might otherwise not encounter another believer that day is a key strategy element.

While traveling through Samaria, Jesus rested at Jacob's well, about the noon hour. It was hot, and Jesus was thirsty. He asked a Samaritan woman who was coming to draw water at the well if she would give him a drink (John 4:4-8). It is curious that the Samaritan woman was coming to draw water at the noon hour, one of the hottest hours of the day. Most others would draw their water during the cooler morning or evening hours. Her choice to go at noon signals that she didn't want anyone to be there when she went to draw her water from the well. Despite her desire to go unnoticed, Jesus, by asking the woman for a drink of water, takes the initiative to open a conversation. His request accomplishes two purposes: he opens a conversation with the woman, and he breaks down established barriers between Jews and Samaritans. The willingness to open conversation with others, to draw them out of their shells in a respectful, friendly way, is an important approach in reaching out to Muslims.

Begin the conversation based on felt needs, whether emotional, physical or social. Your conversation could begin over sports, business, politics or even donated goods. Spiritual conversations do not have to begin on a spiritual topic; they usually begin with a tangible, concrete, day-to-day topic.

Our church began helping refugees from Iraq, providing them with furniture and household items for their apartments. As I was helping deliver a couch to an Iraqi family, the head of the household began a conversation with me on where to place the furniture. He was very grateful for the help from the Christian community and began a discussion on appreciating the political freedoms of the United States. This short conversation began about furniture and ended with me giving him a copy of the Injeel.

Move to a deeper level: The religious level. "The Samaritan woman said to him, 'You are a Jew and I am a Samaritan woman. How can you ask me for a drink?' (For Jews do not associate with Samaritans.)" (John 4:9).

The Samaritan woman is well aware of the social separation between Samaritans and Jews, and yet she still asks Jesus, "How can you ask me for a drink?" Her question is revealing. It shows that she is treating the conversation as a religious discussion because she is comparing Jews and Samaritans. In my experience, I have found it easy to open conversations with Muslims because, like the Samaritan woman, they are already talking about their religion! It's natural for them. I just capitalize on the opportunities God presents. We need not fear opening an exchange about spiritual topics with Muslims, even if it is in a religious setting.

Respond strategically: The miraculous level. "Jesus answered her, 'If you knew the gift of God and who it is that asks you for a drink, you would have asked him and he would have given you living water'" (John 4:10).

Jesus and the Samaritan woman continue their conversation, and Jesus deliberately guides their discussion to a much deeper level. Jesus mastered the art of evangelism. He took the initiative and intentionally maneuvered the conversation to share the good news.

> Jesus mastered the art of evangelism. He took the initiative and intentionally maneuvered the conversation to share the good news.

"Sir," the woman said, "you have nothing to draw with and the well is deep. Where can you get this living water? Are you greater than our father Jacob, who gave us the well and drank from it himself, as did also his sons and his livestock?"

Jesus answered, "Everyone who drinks this water will be thirsty again, but whoever drinks the water I give them will never thirst. Indeed, the water I give them will become in them a spring of water welling up to eternal life."

The woman said to him, "Sir, give me this water so that I won't get thirsty and have to keep coming here to draw water." (John 4:11-15)

The Samaritan woman doesn't exactly "get" what Jesus is suggesting. It is even clearer now that the conversation has turned to religious issues because the Samaritan woman asks Jesus if he is greater than Jacob. Jesus makes her an enticing offer of eternal life, and completely missing the point, she takes it in a literal sense and asks Jesus to give her this living water so that she doesn't have to return to the well. She saw Jesus as a powerful prophet and requested a miracle.

He told her, "Go, call your husband and come back."

"I have no husband," she replied.

Jesus said to her, "You are right when you say you have no husband. The fact is, you have had five husbands, and the man you now have is not your husband. What you have just said is quite true."

"Sir," the woman said, "I can see that you are a prophet. Our ancestors worshiped on this mountain, but you Jews claim that the place where we must worship is in Jerusalem."

"Woman," Jesus replied, "believe me, a time is coming when you will worship the Father neither on this mountain nor in Jerusalem. You Samaritans worship what you do not know; we worship what we do know, for salvation is from the Jews. Yet a time is coming and has now come when the true worshipers will worship the Father in the Spirit and in truth, for they are the kind of worshipers the Father seeks." (John 4:16-23)

Ever patient, Jesus uses a more pointed method of commanding the woman's attention to the heart of the matter. He reveals to her that he is well aware of her personal history. His insight causes her to see Christ as a true prophet, and as such, she feels comfortable conversing about spiritual issues. They begin to discuss how and where one should worship. Jesus ultimately answers, "God is spirit, and his worshipers must worship in the Spirit and in truth" (John 4:24).

The conversation is escalating. It's no longer about the mountain upon which one will worship. Those who worship must worship in *spirit* and *truth*. The Bible is the only book that defines God to humans. God is spirit, and spirit is different from the natural world. We are his creatures and he is the Creator.

The woman said, "I know that Messiah" (called Christ) "is coming. When he comes, he will explain everything to us."
Then Jesus declared, "I, the one speaking to you—I am he." (John 4:25-26)

Jesus reveals to the woman that he is the promised Messiah! He is the Savior, the awaited prophet and leader.

What began as a conversation about water now focuses on God's expectations, salvation from sin, sincere worship and a recognition of who the Messiah is. Rather than wasting conversational space on trivial matters, Christ uses every opportunity to point the Samaritan woman to the truth. Like Jesus, in ministry to Muslims we also must take advantage of the doors God opens for us to develop meaningful, relevant and consequential conversations.

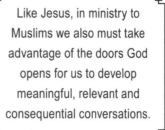

Like Jesus, in ministry to Muslims we also must take advantage of the doors God opens for us to develop meaningful, relevant and consequential conversations.

DRIVING THE CONVERSATION

Typically, our communication process follows a sender-message-receiver model, a relational communication model developed by Wilbur Schramm (see figure 2.1).[2]

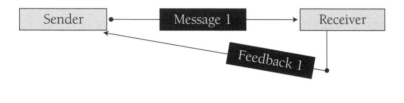

Figure 2.1 Our typical communication

The sender encodes his message into a form the sender understands. The message is in the medium, whether electronic, verbal, written or pictorial. Next, the receiver decodes and interprets the message that results in the receiver sending feedback to the sender. The feedback, in any form, is imperative for the communication process to be effective.

Action Point

Don't waste conversational space on trivial matters! Make all of your conversations point to the Messiah.

For example, it used to be that in television, there was almost no exchange of feedback. But now, with the development of technology and social media, viewers are able to communicate their feedback in real time.

Feedback from the receiver is valuable information that influences both the sender and their message.

As another example, when I speak to large groups, if I see that people are yawning or are turning their heads away, I can tell that the message I am sending is not as engaging as I anticipated. However, if I see people nodding along as I speak or raising hands to answer questions, I know that the audience is interested in the topic. Their feedback helps me to determine how to move the conversation forward.

JESUS' MODEL OF COMMUNICATION

While Schramm's model illustrates the communication process well, Jesus offers us a different model that takes into account how someone can strategically move conversations to a deeper level (see figure 2.2). Christ uses an approach in his dialogue with others in which the sender and the message are at a different spiritual level than the receiver.

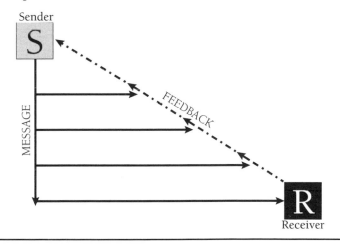

Figure 2.2 Jesus' communication style

In this model, the response or feedback the sender receives is what drives how deep the conversation goes. When the sender receives feedback from the receiver, the sender uses that feedback to guide the conversation to the next level, a more significant level of discussion. Likewise, as the receiver decodes and interprets the message from the sender, the thought process moves into new spiritual understandings. The receiver moves higher in their understanding of spiritual things. The Bible edifies us to think higher than the material world we live in.

In this passage in John, the crucial message Jesus delivers to the Samaritan woman is that he is the Messiah. But he doesn't *start* at that level. He starts with something else, something more tangible and easier to understand. He remains strategic in his approach. How long does the conversation take between Jesus and the Samaritan woman? Fifteen minutes? An hour? It doesn't matter. The point is that over a water well, *Jesus guides their conversation from something physical to a profound spiritual truth.* The amount of time is not the major concern. Instead, the focus is on the person to whom you are speaking and moving the conversation to a higher level of spirituality.

Action Point

Open conversations with Muslims by asking simple questions about their opinions about Christians or what they think about religion. Starting with a topic that is more understandable is less intimidating than starting with a deep theological question.

In ministry to Muslims, such significant conversations may develop quickly or they may take time. Discussion may start about similarities and differences between Muslims and Christians. Maybe then it will progress to "religion." Then maybe the conversation will turn to ideas about God. The purpose is to remain intentional about the topic and approach. There is a tendency to expect that once a message is shared with Muslims, they will respond in a certain way. Not only is this not true, but your greatest concern is not about the specific ways in which Muslims respond, but that you move the conversation to a deeper level.

While I was traveling in Minnesota, I took a taxi, and the driver was from Somalia. There was a good chance that he was Muslim, so I greeted him, "*As-salaamu alaikum!*" and we started chatting. I asked him if he liked being in Minnesota. He replied, "Oh, yes! I hate the cold weather, but it's safe." We laughed about his tongue-in-cheek joke and starting chatting about our likes and dislikes. He finally asked me what I was doing in Minnesota. I said, "I am speaking on how we know that the Bible has not been changed." So now the conversation is moving from about the weather to biblical issues.

"People always tell me," I said, "that humans have changed the Bible. *Astaghfur 'allah!* [God forbid!] How can this be? Who can change the Bible?"

Action Point

Keep a copy of the Injeel on you if possible. You can get an Arabic/English Injeel from www.crescentproject.org/resources.

Although our time was short, the cab driver asked for an Injeel (New Testament). I share this story as an example of how a conversation can plant seeds, moving from a superficial topic to a much more meaningful one. Be strategic and look for those open doors.

SOWING, WATERING AND REAPING

> Just then his disciples returned and were surprised to find him talking with a woman. But no one asked, "What do you want?" or "Why are you talking with her?"
>
> Then, leaving her water jar, the woman went back to the town and said to the people, "Come, see a man who told

me everything I ever did. Could this be the Messiah?" They came out of the town and made their way toward him.

Meanwhile his disciples urged him, "Rabbi, eat something."

But he said to them, "I have food to eat that you know nothing about."

Then his disciples said to each other, "Could someone have brought him food?"

"My food," said Jesus, "is to do the will of him who sent me and to finish his work. Don't you have a saying, 'It's still four months until harvest'? I tell you, open your eyes and look at the fields! They are ripe for harvest." (John 4:27-35)

Jesus' disciples return to him and find him talking with the Samaritan woman. She heads off to town to tell others of her conversation with Jesus. The message he shared is already spreading through her! Jesus ensures that his disciples understand that the food on which he feasts is finishing the Father's work: reaping the harvest.

Even now the one who reaps draws a wage and harvests a crop for eternal life, so that the sower and the reaper may be glad together. Thus the saying "One sows and another reaps" is true. I sent you to reap what you have not worked for. Others have done the hard work, and you have reaped the benefits of their labor. (John 4:36-38)

The fields are ripe for harvesting *now*—not later. The harvest has been ready for two thousand years! Is it time for Muslims to hear the gospel? Absolutely! The message has been ready for two thousand years. We are late to the job! Jesus himself said that the fields are ripe for harvesting. More than that, Jesus says that in the harvest, both the sower and the reaper will rejoice. How can this be? The sower does not see the harvest immediately, so how does he celebrate? He rejoices *by faith*. He waters and cares for the seeds by faith, trusting that those seeds will grow and produce a fruitful harvest. Likewise, the reaper does not see the process or the efforts put into making that harvest possible. But together, the sower and reaper rejoice in the harvest because people were faithful. Today, your role might be as sower, cultivator, waterer or harvester, yet by faith in Christ we rejoice throughout the process.

The harvest has been ready for two thousand years! Is it time for Muslims to hear the gospel? Absolutely! The message has been ready for two thousand years. We are late to the job!

Remember, ministry to Muslims is more like a marathon than a sprint. Keep your focus.

DIVINE APPOINTMENTS

When I leave the country on short-term trips, people encourage me by telling me that they are praying for divine appointments. I say that every appointment—every one—is a divine appointment. With every person I meet, I am either sowing, or watering or reaping. I am entering in on someone else's labor. It is God who set up the process this way, so that we never get the glory for his work. When a Muslim prays with me to receive Christ, it has nothing to do with me. God was already working. Others have been sowing and watering before me. Right now, you might be sowing, you might be watering, or you might be reaping. No matter what you are doing, enjoy the process.

> With every person I meet, I am either sowing or watering or reaping. I am entering in on someone else's labor. It is God who set up the process this way, so that we never get the glory for his work.

Sadly, some Christian organizations send out people with expectations that are not viable or are unbiblical. We set out to plant churches, and then we're completely disappointed when a church isn't planted. Or perhaps the message we have to share is a message like Jonah's: "Repent." That's not exactly a message we want to sign up to share, is it? Everyone wants to be a part of the harvest, but we struggle with the sowing. I believe the reason for the recent revival in Africa is the *years* of sowing that have taken place. People went, sowed, prayed, prayed, sowed, sowed and prayed some more for Africa. Do you think people are not praying for Muslims today? We must continue to pray that God would move among Muslims. Sowing, watering and reaping are all a part of the kingdom of God.

Action Point

Commit to every aspect of the harvesting process. Pray for Muslims. Speak with Muslims. Go deeper in dialogue with Muslims. Share the gospel message with Muslims. And rejoice if you have the privilege of helping to lead a Muslim to a decision to receive Christ.

THEY WILL SPREAD THE NEWS

"Many of the Samaritans from that town believed in him because of the woman's testimony, 'He told me everything I ever did.' So when the Samaritans came to him, they urged him to stay with them, and he stayed two days. And because of his words many more became believers" (John 4:39-41).

Because Jesus was so strategic about his sharing of the good news, the Samaritan woman's testimony of Jesus spread like wildfire. When one person comes to Christ, he can tell his family, or his town, and the gospel continues to spread. When I was speaking in northern Indiana, an audience member boorishly spoke up, citing a statistic that by a particular year there would be more Muslims on the planet than anyone else, and that a Muslim woman would have an average of seven children. I told this young man, "Great. If you win one of those Muslims, then he can tell his siblings. These numbers really just show that there is more potential for more Muslims to come to faith in Jesus."

Remember, there were only twelve disciples. *Twelve!* To me, the belief that numbers, money or politics is going to help the kingdom of God is unfounded. They are tools that God can and will use, but these "supports" are unnecessary. God is already on the move. To engage in compelling evangelism, start with the people God puts into your life. One person, two people. Share with them and see the efforts multiply. You may have a friend who has a friend in Kenya, who has a friend in Tanzania, who has a friend from Pakistan. We don't know how the gospel spreads. Trust that the Lord will use those seeds that you sow.

The Book of Acts clearly expresses this point, affirming that we must never despise small beginnings, for our God is actively building his kingdom on earth. The disciples multiplied through God's power.

I've met countless young people who actively sow seeds in faith. Alex, a Shi'ite young man, lived in California and met some Christian friends. They gave him a copy of the book *Is the Injeel Corrupted?* I spoke with Alex on the phone about the book, and a few months later, I received an email from him stating that he had prayed to receive Christ as his

Action Point

Be intentional about sharing the gospel message with Muslims. You never know how your message to one Muslim could impact an entire community or network of Muslims.

Savior. A few months after that, he called to tell me that his mother was coming to visit him from Tehran. "I'm going to give her a Bible," he said, "and a copy of *Is the Injeel Corrupted?*" We prayed together about his mother's visit. Two months later, right around Thanksgiving, Alex found me online and shared, "Fouad, I just led my mom in the sinner's prayer." God used someone to meet and share the gospel with Alex, who was used to reach his mother, and now Alex is reaching many more Muslims for Christ.

God is on the move. He uses one person to reach another. Trust that you, too, will be called to reach others.

Closing prayer: *Heavenly Father, thank you that you are the master of the harvest. Thank you that you choose to use me. Make me your instrument to lead meaningful conversations with Muslims about salvation. In Christ's name, amen.*

Chapter 3

Compelling Evangelism

Practical Approaches

—●—

STANDING ON THE EDGE of the Mediterranean Sea, enjoying the sunset, a group of American Christian college students were approached by Muslim youths. These young people were students and able to converse in English. Conversations ensued, filled with smiles and laughter as they talked about culture and the latest electronic gadgets. There was a lot of positive communication, but when asked why they were visiting this country, there was a brief awkward silence. What do they say? What is their reason for being there?

This team was trained and prepared. Their answer was that they were there to serve Jesus the Messiah by praying for the people of that nation. The Muslim youth were impressed and grateful for their visit to pray for the nation. The conversation continued as a couple of the students indicated that they were reading the Injeel and had some questions.

Another example is Brian, who serves in central Asia as a teacher. On the second day of arriving at the school, he had lunch with the national principal of the school. The principal asked Brian, "Why are you a Christian?" Knowing the principles of communicating like Jesus, Brian began from that question and shared the good news. After a mere hour conversation, the principal asked for an Injeel. He wanted to study it.

Many Christians serving in Muslim countries or among international students consistently struggle with how to move the conversation to talk about Jesus. How can we make the relationships and the conversations we have with Muslims move into deeper topics rather than staying superficial?

This is why it is imperative that we have a clear understanding of the communication principles of the Messiah. We need to understand the principles and develop a communications toolbox to assist us in effectively seizing the opportunity to represent Christ and his teachings.

In the previous chapter we examined the principles of witnessing like Jesus our Messiah, which are foundational for our communication with Muslims. Our goal in this chapter is the same: to connect Christians and Muslims through effective communication. This chapter will highlight additional ways to begin effective communication.

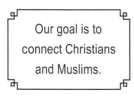

Our goal is to connect Christians and Muslims.

First Peter 3:15 says, "Always be prepared to give an answer to everyone who asks you to give the reason for the hope that you have." Witnessing like Jesus is mastering the art of evangelism—sharing the hope that we have. Our goal from all conversations is to share the hope we have in Christ. Whether we are answering questions or having a casual conversation, the Bible compels us to share about the hope we have.

You already have the Holy Spirit who will empower you. As we examine the life of Christ, we see many methods that he implements to share the good news that we can use to share the good news with our friends and neighbors. It's time to put those methods to work. This chapter will cover biblical approaches that show respect to Muslims and create compelling conversations that lead to the Savior Jesus.

ASK QUESTIONS

We are curious beings, and a lot of people enjoy being asked their opinion on a matter. One approach you can use in conversation with Muslims is to ask strategic questions. They do not have to be serious theological questions; they can be as simple as, "Hey, have you read the Bible?" or "What do you think of Christians?" Asking clarifying questions gives you a way to move the conversation to a deeper level.

- "What do you mean by that?"
- "How do you know that's true?"
- "Where did you get this information?"
- "What happens if the information is wrong?"
- "Have you heard of the Messiah?"
- "Do you have daily peace?"

Our Lord used this in his interaction with people around him. Whether talking with the religious establishment of the day or the average fisherman or the Gentile foreigners, Christ always asked questions and welcomed questions. Christ answered questions to teach the listeners about the kingdom of heaven. Sometimes he answered a question with a question, helping the listener use deduction to arrive at a specific conclusion. Sometimes he even chose not to answer the question, but rather told a story that depicted the concepts of the kingdom of heaven. Questions always help build a relationship and strengthen the conversation. As people respond and connect and share their thoughts, they feel valued and respected.

I was on a radio program speaking about how the Qur'an does not have any descriptions about heaven for women. The only descriptions given about heaven are for men. A Muslim woman called into the program and stated, "A hadith from Muhammad says that heaven is at the feet of mothers."

I responded to her, "What do you mean by that? You say that heaven is at the feet of mothers. What does that mean? You have a large audience listening right now, so it will be great for you to explain it to us. Does it mean that every time a mother takes a step that there's a new heaven starting?"

She replied, "Well, it means that when you're talking to your mother, it's like being in heaven."

I clarified, "So it's about mother-child relationships. He's not talking here about eternity or where Muslim women go in the afterlife."

Action Point

Diffuse anger and arguments in love and with respect by asking questions.

The purpose in asking these kinds of clarifying questions is not to be mean or aggressive. The purpose is for more clarification and to understand what Muslims mean when they make a statement. Muslims are raised to obey without questioning. Asking them critical questions in a respectful way can lead them to think deeply about spiritual matters.

INTEGRATE SCRIPTURE INTO CONVERSATION

Because Islam is very "religious," Muslims have respect for other people who memorize God's Word. Therefore, using Bible verses is an appropriate means of opening up or continuing a conversation. If you have a favorite verse, or have memorized a verse from the Bible, you can feel free to share it with your Muslim friends. It very well may spark their interest.

I did this when I was at the eye doctor with my son in Lebanon. While in the waiting room, a Muslim man told us about his wife, who was having some eye problems. He concluded his story by sharing a verse from the Qur'an. I responded in turn with a verse from the Bible, Romans 8:28, that in all things God works for the good of those who love him. His eyes opened wide, and he said, "Does the Injeel say something that beautiful?" It was an amazing moment. We were just sitting in a doctor's waiting room, and suddenly this man wanted to know more about the Injeel. Use Bible verses to drive the conversation to a deeper level.

Share Your Personal Testimonies

What did God do for you yesterday? Maybe he answered a request you had been praying about. When you're having coffee with a Muslim friend, or a new Muslim acquaintance, share your testimony of what God has done for you. This is a way of spreading the gospel in a personal way, much like how the Samaritan woman shared her personal testimony with others in town. Such testimonies don't have to be about how you were saved. They can be as straightforward as God's answering a prayer, or how he worked in a situation for you. These testimonies can give others ideas about how the Lord works in our lives personally.

Your personal testimony of faith in Christ as your personal Savior has a lasting impact on people. The Bible is clear that following Jesus is a personal decision that is lived out daily. The Messiah Jesus asked people to follow him. Following Christ is a decision of the heart and will. I love hearing personal testimonies of faith because they show the greatness and creativity of God the Father in leading people to Christ the Savior. I encourage you to always share with others why you are a follower of Christ. Your testimony is your story, and others cannot dispute God's work in your life. By sharing your story, you are sharing God's story, and he is glorified. Sharing your personal experience with God will help Muslims see that the God of the Bible is approachable and personal.

While sharing the gospel in southern Spain, I met a young Moroccan called Khaled. Khaled began a spiritual conversation once he found out that I am an Injeeli (a follower of the Injeel). He began with the usual attacks on the authenticity of the Bible and why the Qur'an was revealed to replace the Bible. (I will be dealing with that question later in this book.) While talking to this sharp young man, I felt the Spirit of God compelling me to share my personal testimony. I began sharing how God saved me from the sin of hate. How God gave me love for all my neighbors and enemies. How God changed my value system so that today I pray for the Palestinian and Israeli people.

> The Bible is clear that following Jesus is a personal decision that is lived out daily.

He listened intently. He exclaimed that he had read the Qur'an twice and found no cure for sin. My response was that Jesus is the only cure for sin. Sinners need a Savior. Those dead in sin need to come alive through the Messiah, who rose from the dead. He alone can give all people the power to live a godly life.

Khaled gladly received the Injeel. He and I continued our conversation on what it means to follow Christ and accept him as Savior. My personal testimony was a proof of God's work in my life regardless of my background. Likewise, God can work in Khaled's life regardless of his background.

Dawn was an American believer who went on a missions trip with Crescent Project. During the training she confided with her trainer that she does not feel adequate, theologically or religiously, to connect with Muslims and communicate effectively. Part of our training at Crescent Project is to help believers share their personal testimony in an effective way with their Muslim friends.

Dawn felt relieved that she can share her testimony and that is sufficient for God to use in impacting Muslims. Dawn grasped the concept that she is serving as an ambassador and that all believers have a testimony—a story of how they came to faith in Christ. Dawn became courageous and shared with many Muslims in her college community. Dawn even served on multiple overseas ministry trips where she shared the gospel with many Muslims through her personal testimony of faith in Christ.

TELL STORIES

Creating stories or telling notable stories you have heard can open up conversations through the use of metaphor. Stories can be a nonthreatening tool to encourage others to share their opinions because, after all, it's just a story. Right?

In the Middle East, talking about politics can sometimes lead to less than civil conversations. So to prevent a dinner party from going sour, a friend of mine tells a story about a tailor who had a bird in a cage. On a daily basis, the tailor would hit the cage with a stick and not feed the bird. Of course, under that kind of treatment, the bird was always scared. One day, a rich man purchased that bird from the tailor and brought the bird to his garden, which was filled with birds of all kinds. But the bird wouldn't leave its cage because it was so scared. Every day, the other birds would flock to the bird's cage and say, "Come out! The best thing is to eat grain right from the hands of the king."

That's where the story ends. My friend then asks the others at the dinner party, "What do you think this story means?" This begins a spiritual conversation.

Move the conversation intentionally!

Bible stories are also a rich source of truth and narrative. Think about sharing the story of Jonah, Noah, David or Abraham and his sacrifice. The story of John the Baptist is even found in

the Qur'an and can be a key text in reaching out to Muslims
because the story is all about preparing the way for Jesus! "Look,
the Lamb of God!" (John 1:29).

> The Qur'an mentions the coming of John the Baptist.
> John is considered a prophet in Islam and is called Yahya.
> See Qur'an 3:39; 6:85; 19:7-15; 21:90.

Many of the prophets of the Old Testament are mentioned by
name in the Qur'an. Sadly, the Qur'an does not describe their life,
and many Muslim scholars lack details on the life of many of these
prophets. Using the stories about the prophets is a great way to
inform Muslims of valuable spiritual information that they have
never heard. Many Muslims seek to know more about what the
Bible says about these prophets. These stories reveal many spiritual
concepts that can help our communication with Muslims go deeper.

One such story is of Abraham, when he was asked to offer his
son as a sacrifice. The richness of the story and its details compel
Muslims to know more. Many Muslims grasp the idea of a redeemer, as they understand the details of the son of Abraham
being freed because the ram was a replacement sacrifice.[1]

Parables. Parables are yet another valuable source of stories,
and these are stories loaded with teaching. Consider sharing the
parable of the prodigal son, the Pharisee and the tax collector,
the lost son, the lost sheep, or Lazarus and the rich man. Parables are both culturally relevant and accessible. A theological
text can be easily forgotten, but the meaning of a parable is
passed down over thousands of years. Parables are still a form of
communication used in many countries of the world. Parables
in the Bible, with their Jewish and Mediterranean flavor, connect
to the hearts of the listeners.

Read the parables of Jesus (see appendix 1 for a complete list). Choose a couple of parables that you personally appreciate. Memorize the story, its characters and message—this is the fastest way to share it. With your own words, you can retell the parable to your Muslim friends. I would even recommend finding a present-day equivalent you can use to show the meaning of this parable.

A friend of mine is serving in Nigeria and has found that the parables connect with the whole family, parents and children at the same time. His joy is when the children understand the spiritual meaning before the adults. Communicating the gospel becomes more effective when paired with the words of Jesus in a parable.

While visiting San Antonio, I had the opportunity to meet five students from Afghanistan. As we talked over a cup of tea, I shared the story of the Pharisee and the tax collector. Once I shared the prayer of the self-righteous Pharisee, the conversation took a different turn. All the Afghans wanted to know how to please God. Who can please God? The message was clear that only God is righteous and all of us are sinners. God is pleased with a repentant heart that seeks salvation from God. Sharing Christ as the Redeemer and Savior was a natural transition from sharing that parable.

Proverbs. Proverbs and idioms are other means of storytelling. It is both relevant and appropriate to use proverbs from the Bible as well as cultural proverbs. In Lebanon, we use the proverb "*Eid wehde ma bit za'ef*," meaning, "One hand cannot clap." It means that you need another hand to do things in life. This proverb can be used to illustrate how Jesus can be that other hand. Learning idioms in other languages can open doors to having new conversations with Muslims. All cultures have idioms—learning your friends' culture and asking about idioms will deepen your conversations and help you communicate effectively.

A friend of mine from England has served for ten years with a Muslim people group. He has learned their idioms, proverbs and poetry. It is a joy for me to see him open conversations about the good news by sharing a proverb or a cultural idiom.

These are not the only ways to reach Muslims.

Psalms. God has given us a treasure of promises in the psalms. The book of Psalms is culturally relevant, and its poetic structure appeals to Muslims. Use the psalms to communicate God's promises and reveal his character.

Nancy is a Christian student at a major university. Nancy became friends with Fatima from Saudi Arabia. Fatima decided to take a trip back home and perform the Hajj, the Islamic ritual of visiting the Ka'aba. During the Hajj, Fatima was caught in a stampede and miraculously escaped death. She shared with Nancy that she now has nightmares and fears for the future. Nancy shared with her Psalms 23 and 91 to encourage her to have faith in God. Fatima enjoys reading the psalms. She has her own Bible now and loves reading the promises of God in the psalms.

GIVE GIFTS

Gift giving can deepen our conversations and relationships with Muslims. A gift shows appreciation and creates a memory of an event and the relationship you have with that person. A gift will increase the trust between you and your Muslim friend and establish a value for the relationship. Gift giving also creates a mood of generosity. It is a great way to be generous with our time and money. Most cultures encourage reciprocation in gift giving.

However, gift giving must be done wisely so it will not distract from our goal of communicating the gospel. Give a gift that has a meaning for both cultures. Give a gift from a special time you had, a sporting event, a conference, a trip or a book. Always give the Injeel as a gift. To us Christians, it is the best gift of all. Make gift giving a regular practice.

Haytham was a devout Shia Muslim. While traveling on vacation in Europe he was hosted and befriended by a Spanish couple. The couple showed true biblical hospitality and offered him an Injeel. Haytham had heard of the Injeel and was eager to read it. As Haytham read the Injeel he was struck by the uniqueness and beautiful words of Jesus. Haytham's life was changed when he read, "Blessed are the pure in heart, for they will see God" (Matthew 5:8). A year later Haytham was baptized as a follower of Christ.

PRAY

Prayer changes things. God repeatedly asks us in his Word to pray. He yearns for us to pray and ask (Matthew 7:7). God is moving on this earth because his righteous servants are praying. So pray continually (1 Thessalonians 5:17).

Ritualistic prayer is an important part of Islam. For that reason, we need to consider witnessing to Muslims by praying both for them and with them. Many Muslims today are afraid. They fear Allah's (Arabic for *God*) wrath, demonic activity, shaming their family, Judgment Day and the future. As believers in Christ, we do not fear tomorrow, for Jesus is the same yesterday, today and forever. We need to pray for our Muslim friends by name. If you do not know any Muslims, pray for the Muslim world.

Action Point

Crescent Project is challenging Christians to pray for Muslims every Friday at noon. Join in that commitment by signing up at www.crescentproject.org/prayer.

In the last ten years Muslims have been very open to Christian workers' praying for them and their needs. Many appreciate the prayer. If your Muslim friend or neighbor has a need, ask if you can pray together for God to meet that need. Pray and boldly ask God in the name of the Savior Jesus. We have a special relationship with God—he is our heavenly Father. Praying with Muslims gives you opportunities to pray for them by name and to know what is on their hearts. Use these times to build a strong, personal relationship with your friend—a relationship that is modeled on the relationship our Lord and Savior has with us.

PRACTICE HOSPITALITY

The dictionary definition of hospitality focuses on pleasantly receiving guests by offering them a welcoming environment. However, biblical hospitality focuses on *loving* and *serving*. It goes much deeper than simply offering a welcoming environment. In today's world, getting ahead and being around influential people is important. Inviting a public figure or other popular person to dinner would certainly be a momentous occasion. But biblical hospitality says to do the very opposite! "When you give a banquet, invite the poor, the crippled, the lame, the blind, and you will be blessed. Although they cannot repay you, you will be repaid at the resurrection of the righteous" (Luke 14:13-14). The idea of hospitality here is not about an even exchange of appreciation for those who would reciprocate. It is about serving those in need, those who are marginalized.

Ali was a Sunni Muslim student from Saudi Arabia. Coming to the United States to study was a very difficult thing for him. His English was weak and he was a very religious young man. He had performed the Hajj and had very little tolerance for any of the perceived pagan rituals of the American Christians.

Upon arrival in America, a Christian family who hosted him for more than two years welcomed him. Their hospitality, acts of service and kindness made him wonder what was so different about these Americans that he didn't see in other citizens. His curiosity was heightened when they shared with him that they were practicing believers in Christ. Ali began reading the Injeel. Though it took time, Ali concluded that true believers in Christ do not have pagan rituals and do not hate Muslims. He found out that true Christians love Muslims and are hospitable people.

This family's hospitality impacted Ali and drew him to faith in Christ. Ali's journey to faith took some time, but it began with the influence of a Christian couple who practiced biblical hospitality.

God reminds us that we must treat foreigners as those who are native-born. We are called to love our neighbors as ourselves (Leviticus 19:34; Matthew 22:39). Such love can speak volumes to our Muslim friends.

I want to be clear that I am not generalizing that all Muslims have physical or material needs, or that all Muslims are marginalized, or even that all Muslims are foreigners. But we do know that Muslims have a very clear need of the Savior. Practical ways to be hospitable include having Muslims over for coffee or dinner, or taking the time to visit them in their homes. Offer your time and invest in personal relationships with Muslims, having compelling conversations with them so that they, too, may know Jesus. Show them the "unusual kindness" the apostles experienced (Acts 28:2). For when we serve others by offering them hospitality, we serve Christ (Colossians 3:23-24).

BE INTENTIONAL

During my first trip to Morocco, I thoroughly enjoyed the beauty of the country and the hospitality of the people. We took Bibles with us and talked with all kinds of people during the trip. If someone asked for a Bible, we gave it to them—but only if they asked for it. In the marketplace in Marrakesh, my friend Mark wanted to get a *galaba*, the traditional Moroccan cultural dress and headdress. The shopkeeper we found had a long beard down to the second button on his shirt. I greeted him with the traditional Islamic greeting, "As-salaam alaikum," and explained what my friend was looking for. In Arabic, the shopkeeper asked me if my friend was Australian. Confused, I told him, "No, he's American."

The shopkeeper picked up a dagger from the table, unsheathed it, and put its point to my friend's chest. "What if I stick this in your heart?" he asked in English.

Wide-eyed, I told the shopkeeper, "My brother, we're Arabs. We're supposed to be hospitable."

The shopkeeper sheathed the dagger again and said in English, "Oh, I was just kidding." After purchasing the items, we left the shop, and Mark and I took a moment to pray for the shopkeeper. We didn't know his name, but we prayed for him.

On my next trip to Morocco a year later, we went again to Marrakesh. I looked for the same shopkeeper. He was in the same store, but his beard was trimmed because the king had banned any outward signs of fanaticism. I asked him if he remembered me from a year ago. He didn't recall me immediately, so I asked him his name. He said "Adel," which is my father's name. We started talking about my last trip, and he asked me what I do. I said I do a lot of teaching about the Bible and the Qur'an. He said, "I read the book of Luke. Can you get me the whole Injeel?" Surprised that he somehow read the book of Luke, I said sure, and I gave him a copy of the Arabic New Testament as a gift.

On my third trip to Morocco, we were in Marrakesh again.

Action Point

Follow up with the people with whom you've shared Christ. This lets them see that you care for them.

What do you think I did? I looked for Adel; I'd been praying for him for a year. I found him again in his same shop and greeted him. He shook my hand and asked me, "Who are you?" I reminded him about our meeting the previous year, and he said again that he meets a lot of people. In a hushed voice, trying not to attract attention, I prompted him, "I gave you a gift . . . you know . . . the book of Jesus."

He said aloud, "Oh, yes, the book of Jesus!" The two assistants in the shop whipped their heads around, saying, "What? The book of Jesus?"

Trying to diffuse the unwanted attention, I told Adel I wanted to look at an item on the other side of the store. But I also asked him, "Adel, are you reading the Injeel?"

He said, "Yes, I'm reading it, but I have a lot of questions. Is there someone who can help me understand?"

I said, "Of course." I called a friend who was a pastor, and he connected Adel with a local believer. The gift I offered him turned out to be a watershed moment in Adel's life. Do not be afraid to give a gift. The best gifts you can give to another are the words of Jesus.

Intentionality has the power to move hearts—hearts that may one day worship the Lord, from all over the world. "After this I looked, and there before me was a great multitude that no one could count, from every nation, tribe, people and language, standing before the throne and before the Lamb. They were wearing white robes and were holding palm branches in their hands" (Revelation 7:9). Make no mistake. Muslims will be there. But we must go the distance in reaching out to them.

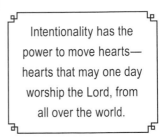

> Intentionality has the power to move hearts— hearts that may one day worship the Lord, from all over the world.

Are you ready to take that step? I am sure you are. I pray that your communication toolbox is being filled. There are more tools to come. May God use these tools in your life and ministry to Muslims.

> Closing prayer: *Our heavenly Father, thank you for your Holy Spirit that works in the hearts of all people. Fill me with your Spirit and empower me to use these tools to build bridges with Muslims—bridges that will lead them to see the risen Christ. In his name I pray, amen.*

Chapter 4

Bridge-Building Approaches

—●—

A Bridge Across the Chasm

In chapter 1, we saw that a chasm separates you from your Muslim friends and neighbors. You stand on the side of Christ's forgiveness, while Muslims stand on the side of guilt, uncertainty and fear. Your goal as a Christian is to build a bridge for your friends to cross from fear to faith.

Your Muslim friends desperately need your sympathy and compassion; their religion falls sadly short in addressing their deepest human needs. You have the opportunity to smooth the rough places in their understanding of God. Devout Muslims pray to God daily, "Show us the straight path." Jesus says, "I am the way" (John 14:6). He is the path that Muslims need. Could it be that God is calling you to clear the way for Jesus to enter the life of your Muslim friend? Only Christ can answer the plea of Muslims worldwide and lead them in the straight path.

Being an Ambassador of Christ

When we reach out to Muslims—or anyone!—we are not going in our own name, in the name of a missions organization or in the name of a church. Remember, we are going in the name of

Jesus Christ, who said, "All authority in heaven and on earth has been given to me" (Matthew 28:18). Therefore, because we are called by Jesus to reach out to those who do not know him, we take the initiative in ministering to others in the confidence that Christ will work on our behalf. But *we* must take initiative. I believe there is a day coming when Muslims will come to our churches, asking us to tell them about Jesus. This is already starting to happen. I received a call from a church in Washington, DC. An Iranian woman showed up at the building, asking for someone to tell her about Jesus. Those days are few and far between, but they are coming. Until that day, we are compelled to "go."

In 2 Corinthians 5:20, the Bible says, "We are therefore Christ's ambassadors, as though God were making his appeal through us." An ambassador represents a country—an ambassador does *not* make people citizens of that country. You are an ambassador of Jesus. *You* do not make people citizens of heaven. Isn't that a freeing concept? We have neither the power nor the authority to make people citizens of heaven. Reaching out to Muslims has nothing to do with how many people pray with me to receive Christ. It is about how many people I have represented Christ to that day. If we share Christ with all Muslims and they all say no, then they all say no. Many people have rejected the message. It's tragic, but it's ultimately their responsibility. No matter the results, we are to continue to be ambassadors for Jesus.

> An ambassador represents a country—an ambassador does *not* make people citizens of that country. You are an ambassador of Jesus. *You* do not make people citizens of heaven.

Being an ambassador is not always an easy job. One of the most depressing conversations I remember having was with a man who was a missionary to North Africa. I was telling him that I was sensing a call to devote my life to reaching out to Muslims. In response, he threw his arm around my shoulder and said, "Fouad, let me tell you something. I have spent ten years reaching out to Muslims, and I have seen two people convert."

I thought, "Well, that's disappointing. Ten years and only two converts. What a bummer."

But then the Lord spoke to me. "What if one of those two converts becomes a Billy Graham to North Africa?"

Being an ambassador is not about the numbers—it's about reaching out to Muslims, sharing Christ, loving them and representing his teaching. Today, thousands of Muslims are reading the words of Jesus. Thousands have made a profession of faith in Christ as the Messiah. Thousands have been baptized. Muslims are responding like never before.

Christ's ambassador knows the starting point. So where does an ambassador begin? If you've ever seen the comedy duo Abbott and Costello's "Who's on First" skit, you've seen how two people can use the same words but seem to be speaking two different languages. A Christian and a Muslim also come to a conversation with quite different sets of assumptions about each other and their cultures. The same words and concepts—like God, *good, devotion* and *freedom*—may be rife with dissimilar meanings. You might walk away from such a conversation believing you've communicated clearly with your Muslim

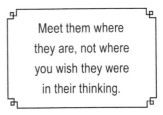

Meet them where they are, not where you wish they were in their thinking.

friend, when in reality he or she comes away believing you meant something radically different from what you intended.

Part of speaking the same "language" as your Muslim friend is to understand their current worldview and assumptions about God and themselves, and you and your culture. You need to meet them where they are, not where you wish they were in their thinking. If they are going to move toward a relationship with Christ, some of their beliefs about God, themselves and life will need to change drastically, but that will not necessarily happen overnight. Pray for a heart that respects their beliefs, but also pray for patient love that longs to guide them into God's kingdom of light.

Action Point

Do your homework. Read up on Muslim and Arab culture. Learn from your Muslim friends about their traditional meals, clothing and customs. Inquire about their beliefs about their world. Be curious. Your respectful questions may lead to a deeper conversation!

Among the beliefs that you first need to recognize and gently try to change are their misconceptions about Christians and Christianity. If you try to explain the good news without first removing these obstacles, your Muslim friend is likely to stay stuck in an attitude of disrespect for all Western Christians, including you.

Most Muslims have never met an authentic follower of Jesus. They assume that whatever they see in Western media represents typical Christian behavior and standards. Even when Muslims come to the United States, Canada or Europe, they are so insulated in their Islamic community that their negative stereotypes endure. They do not know what true life in Jesus can look like.

Muslims are not merely uninformed, living in a truth vacuum—they're actively *mis*informed about our faith,

Action Point

Live a life that goes above and beyond what other people see on TV. Your integrity is a silent message to all about your character.

taught errors and falsehoods about Christianity. And since most have no means of verifying or refuting what they're taught, they don't know any different. Fortunately, we all have opportunities to enlighten Muslims living right around us.

When I was sharing with a Muslim man, he said to me, "You Christians worship three gods."

I corrected him politely, "No, sir, we worship only one God."

Twice more he asserted that I worship three gods, and finally I could take it no longer. "Excuse me, sir. If you want to teach me Islam, I will listen and respect you. But do not teach me Christianity."

You can see that interacting with Muslims takes a measure of grace and compassion. Not only must we share truth, but we must often first correct the beliefs they hold about us that are simply not true. "But do this with gentleness and respect," as the Bible exhorts us (1 Peter 3:15). For this reason, Christlike attitudes of patience, compassion, kindness and empathy must clothe us as we share truth with Muslims. Without love, the truth can feel like an attack.

Christ's ambassador knows his or her identity. One foundational prerequisite to witnessing to Muslims is often ignored or passed by in our zeal to reach out to Muslims and train others to do the same. It's the issue of salvation. Not the Muslim's, but *yours.*

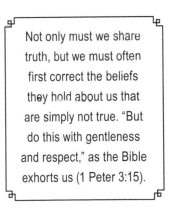

Not only must we share truth, but we must often first correct the beliefs they hold about us that are simply not true. "But do this with gentleness and respect," as the Bible exhorts us (1 Peter 3:15).

What does it mean to be saved? It means to belong to Jesus in every way. Jesus said, "Whoever wants to be my disciple must deny themselves and take up their cross daily and follow me" (Luke 9:23). To be saved means to sell out to Jesus, committing yourself in every way to following his commands. An unsaved person cannot bear witness to Christ's redeeming power; a person cannot represent a leader he or she does not follow.

To be saved means to be assured of your destination—to know where you are going. Some claim that such certainty is arrogance. But it isn't arrogant to be sure of your salvation when you know you didn't earn it, when you know that it is based solely on the price that Jesus paid and the promises he has made. He says, "Very truly I tell you, whoever hears my word and believes him who sent me has eternal life and will not be judged but has crossed over from death to life" (John 5:24).

When you are saved, you are also indwelt with the Holy Spirit of God and given gifts of the Spirit. Just as Jesus breathed on his first disciples and said, "Receive the Holy Spirit" (John 20:22), he still breathes on his followers today, empowering them to live for him and testify about him. Assurance of your salvation implies your full, continual acceptance of God's power and resources, along with the willingness to exercise them according to his will every moment of every day.

Action Point

Continue to study the Word faithfully and to pray fervently. You will be continually refreshed by your encounters with the Lord and energized to share what you are learning with your Muslim friends.

As an ambassador, you must first ask yourself, *Am I truly following Jesus?* If the answer is yes, you should already see the characteristics of Christ evident in your life, in both large and small ways. You should see yourself inevitably growing into the character of Jesus, as God's child and representative.

Don't let your allegiance be divided or distracted by theological differences with other Christians. You belong to Christ, and your

Muslim friend should leave the conversation knowing more about Christ, not a particular church denomination. Many times before a spiritual conversation with a Muslim, I will pray to be filled with the Holy Spirit and focused simply and purely on Jesus: "Lord Jesus, I am ready to share about you. Open and guide the discussion." Through prayer, you align your ambitions with Christ's ambitions, you acknowledge your dependence on him, and you allow him to prepare you to share.

> You belong to Christ, and your Muslim friend should leave the conversation knowing more about Christ, not a particular church denomination.

Christ's ambassador is loving. My friend Muhammad was born in the Middle East but moved to America as a small child. When he was a teenager, he became a fanatic for Islam and wanted to spread the message of Islam and its superiority to people of all other religions. Every Friday he went to the masjid (mosque or Islamic center) and prayed and listened to the *khutba* (Islamic sermon). Two days later, every Sunday, he went to church to debate with the Christians and show them the errors of their ways. Each time, the pastor tried to answer Muhammad's questions and objections with love. Five years later, when Muhammad made a commitment to follow Christ and accept him as his Savior, he was asked why he stepped out to follow Christ. "I could not get over how much they loved me," he said. "I was being so nasty to Christians, yet they were so kind to me."

> When Muhammad made a commitment to follow Christ and accept him as his Savior, he was asked why he stepped out to follow Christ. "I could not get over how much they loved me," he said. "I was being so nasty to Christians, yet they were so kind to me."

One intrinsic component of the character of Christ's ambassador is the unconditional love of Jesus—love that blesses when cursed, prays when mistreated. It is love like the pastor showed, love that responds to a nasty accusation with kind words and prays earnestly for a nondefensive response and for eyes to see the pain beneath the antagonism. Arguments and debates stop dead in their tracks when faced with compassion. The love of God is stronger than the hatred of men.

Action Point

Love Muslims by continually showing them respect and by remaining on friendly terms. Your love for them may help to change their hearts for eternity.

This is not the romantic love that Hallmark markets so effectively in the month of February. And it is not merely a humanitarian love, where we hold hands and sing "Kumbaya" and go home. No, it is the love that looks someone in the face and says, "I love you no matter what." Jesus gives the power to love in this way. That doesn't mean we agree with our Muslim friends in all things; it means we accept them where they are, but we love them too much to let them stay there. And we pray earnestly that they will be changed by the life and teachings of Christ. Islam is devoid of such unconditional love. Most Muslims don't understand the love God has for them—love that gives to the point of sacrifice, reaching even to the worst of sinners.

> The love of God is stronger than the hatred of men.

Christ's ambassador is friendly. Cultivating a heart of compassion toward Muslims will pave the path of friendliness. Unconditional love helps you create an environment conducive to friendship. It doesn't mean you'll be best friends with the next

Muslim you meet, but you can take measures to foster an atmosphere where Muslims feel at ease and respected.

Our role is not to embarrass Muslims, but to respect them and accept them. *Do not criticize Islam, Muslims or their prophet Muhammad.* Muslims know that their religion and their governments have problems, and sometimes they will point these out themselves. They know Islam doesn't work. They know the Muslim world is a social mess. But they've never heard of a better alternative. As Christ's ambassador, you are to present that alternative. Your role is to represent Christ and to be a friend, not an antagonist.

Muslims come to Christ when they see his glory, power and pure character. His ambassadors must lift him up and showcase his

Action Point

We know that when we feel uncomfortable around a person, we're not willing to hear what they have to say. Strive to create a friendly environment in which your Muslim friend knows he or she can ask you any question, and it will be answered in love.

beauty. Therefore, to create an environment in which you can share this good news, *don't argue.* If you become defensive and respond with harsh words, your Muslim friend will only remember that you argued. It is far better to lose the argument and win the person.

Friendship also requires a consistent time investment, even if it's small. A gospel grenade—lobbing the good news from a relational distance and running away in the opposite direction—is rarely effective. Muslims are watching Christians. They're waiting to see if Christians are for real, if we are living out our faith. They look to see if Christ really can change lives and bring hope. Our time investment, whether big or small, demands that we as ambassadors of Jesus model his teachings. Muslims need to see that we're authentic followers of Jesus.

Christ's ambassador builds bridges. As an ambassador among Muslims, you should have a bridge-building approach, leveraging similarities to communicate truth and bring your friend from an old place to a new place spiritually.

Bridging is simple: Take a concept or practice that is similar—some commonality that is shared by both Islam and Christianity—and use it to build a bridge. Note that commonality means similar, not the *same.* For instance, piety in Islam and Christianity has similarities but also vast differences. Muslims and Christians both consider prayer part of piety. But pious prayer to a Muslim must include a ritual washing of one's hands, face and arms beforehand, and repetitious verses from the Qur'an. Christian prayer is considered pious if it relates personally to God and expresses what is on the believer's heart. They are similar, but not the same.

> Muslims and Christians both consider prayer part of piety. But pious prayer to a Muslim must include a ritual washing of one's hands, face and arms beforehand, and repetitious verses from the Qur'an. Christian prayer is considered pious if it relates personally to God and expresses what is on the believer's heart. They are similar, but not the same.

There are many similarities around which we can develop spiritual conversations with our Muslim friends and acquaintances. We all agree that we worship one God, that God has spoken through his prophets, and that God sent Jesus. But while many practices and concepts between the two are *similar,* the understanding and practice of these is often vastly different.

I once was sharing with Ahmad, a computer engineer, and noticed he would grow visibly tense when I talked about Jesus being our sacrifice or Redeemer. So I prayed silently on the spot and shifted the discussion to history and politics. Out of the blue Ahmad asked me, "Fouad, aren't you afraid of genies?"

I stopped in my tracks. "What do you mean?" I asked him.

"Aren't you afraid of genies appearing in the night and choking you to death?" he asked anxiously. As it turned out, Ahmad's grandfather was a village sheikh who was knee-deep in the occult. He would cast spells and chant the Qur'an to ward off genies (jinn) for villagers.

Here was my chance to build a bridge to the gospel in a way he could understand. I started from a place of common ground, a similarity between our faiths, and moved beyond. He and I both believed in powerful spirit beings—some of them evil. I also took advantage of another commonality, the prophetic authority of Jesus. "I believe in the prophet Jesus," I began. "I pray to Jesus, and he will protect me." I shared more about how Jesus is the Word of God (a title found in the Qur'an, so Muslims agree with it—this was another commonality). Since he is the Word of God, Jesus can do whatever God can do. I invited my friend to come under the protection of Christ, the only one who conquered sin, Satan and death.

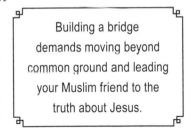

Building a bridge demands moving beyond common ground and leading your Muslim friend to the truth about Jesus.

What started out as a tense discussion ended in an opportunity to create a bridge to the gospel. Ahmad was not moved by my talk about Jesus the Redeemer, but Jesus the Protector hit the bull's-eye for him. Building a bridge demands moving beyond common ground and leading your Muslim friend to the truth about Jesus.

Christ's ambassador is biblical. Remaining biblical is arguably the most important attitude of an ambassador for Jesus. I always use the Injeel in my interactions with Muslims, because the Word of God gives life and changes hearts. It does what I can never do.

Memorize a few verses and use them in conversations with your Muslim friends. Remember, because Muslims grow up honoring the recitation of the Qur'an, they respect followers of Jesus who recite the Word of God.

Action Point

Be diligent to help Muslims cross the bridge to faith in the Messiah.

Rebecca memorized just one verse in Arabic and shared it with an Arabic-speaking Muslim storeowner: "Come to me, all you who are weary and burdened, and I will give you rest. Take my yoke upon you and learn from me, for I am gentle and humble in heart, and you will find rest for your souls" (Matthew 11:28-29). Prior to this, the merchant had paid little attention to her, only speaking to her husband to complete each transaction. But one day she asked if she could speak a blessing to him. He shrugged and said, "Sure, why not?" My friend recited one memorized verse, and it left the man speechless. He was taken aback that a woman would have such a powerful message for him. The Word of God speaks for itself.

Every Friday, Muslims may hear the Qur'an chanted and discussed, but they are likely not familiar at all with the words of Jesus. Make use of the written Word of God, the Bible. It is powerful and speaks with the authority of the Almighty; it will

Action Point

Don't be shy about courteously integrating Scripture into conversation. Muslims respect those who memorize verses from their holy book. Use these opportunities to share the words of Jesus with them.

bring life to your Muslim friends. "My word that goes out from my mouth . . . will not return to me empty, but will accomplish what I desire and achieve the purpose for which I sent it" (Isaiah 55:11).

Christ's ambassador is an example. It's fairly obvious why gospel grenades rarely work. The other side of the coin is failed "friendship evangelism." I knew a Christian who had been friends with a Muslim girl her age for over a year.

"Does your Muslim friend know that you follow Christ?" I asked her.

"Well," the girl said, "we haven't gotten to that yet."

I pushed her further. "Do you want to share with her about Jesus?"

She hesitated. "If I told her now that I'm a Christian, I don't think she would be my friend anymore. I can't risk that."

Many times we falter when only using friendship evangelism because we prioritize our friendship over Jesus' mandate to us as his ambassadors. In an effort not to "impose our beliefs," we never expose our friend to Christ. This young lady had established a welcoming environment, but the subject never turned to Jesus and his teachings.

Christ's strategy was *lifestyle evangelism*. "Jesus went through all the towns and villages, teaching in

> Following Jesus is always about taking the initiative. It's always about sowing widely in every part of life (work, school, neighborhood, clubs and shopping) and by every available means (using words, modeling deeds and personifying Christlike attitudes).

their synagogues, proclaiming the good news of the kingdom and healing every disease and sickness" (Matthew 9:35). He knew that people were both listening to his words and watching his actions. He consistently sowed seeds of the gospel. Using every opportunity and method to share the message of the kingdom, Jesus purposefully lived to sow widely and reap abundantly.

Following Jesus is always about taking the initiative. It's always about sowing widely in every part of life (work, school, neighborhood, clubs and shopping) and by every available means (using words, modeling deeds and personifying Christlike attitudes). Too often when Christians practice friendship evangelism with Muslims, days become weeks, weeks become months, and months become years, and we never overcome our timidity to bring up the name of Jesus. Lifestyle evangelism, following the pattern of Jesus, helps us avoid both gospel grenades and fruitless friendship by enabling us to sow widely, water deeply and harvest abundantly.

> Lifestyle evangelism, following the pattern of Jesus, helps us avoid both gospel grenades and fruitless friendship by enabling us to sow widely, water deeply and harvest abundantly.

BRIDGE BUILDING 101

In addition to the necessary ambassador qualities discussed so far in this chapter, here are a few of the subtle but critically important how-tos in building bridges with Muslims.

1. Always start by praying. Even if all you have is two seconds, silently ask God to bless the other person and to open the discussion for you to share the gospel.

2. Ask for the Holy Spirit to fill your heart and mind. Jesus promised that the Holy Spirit would give us power to be his witnesses: "You will receive power when the Holy Spirit comes on you" (Acts 1:8). Take a moment to acknowledge the Spirit's presence and power, and renew an attitude of dependence and expectation. Confess any sin that hinders your walk and ask God to fill you with his Holy Spirit.

3. *Gather basic information.* Know your new friend's name, country of origin and any other basics. At the least, this is one way of showing interest in the other person. You never know how one bit of information might open a door for you to share, or might lead the other person to deeper openness about themselves.

4. *Be straightforward.* Present your faith in a straightforward manner. Muslims are very open to discussing spiritual issues, and Jesus is a famous and highly respected prophet. Sometimes Muslims ask me, "Are you Muslim or Christian?" I reply, "I am a practicing Christian." Sometimes I reply, "I'm a follower of Christ" or "I'm a muslim through Jesus." Because the word *muslim* means "one who surrenders," I'm telling them I have truly surrendered to God through Jesus. My favorite is to say I am an Injeeli, a person committed to the Injeel. Muslims appreciate commitment—when you respect them, they respect you. Make your response clear! You are a Christian! You belong to Jesus!

5. *Speak with a smile.* You can say practically anything if you are smiling. Even if you receive criticism, keep smiling. Behind most criticisms you'll find misunderstanding, so try not to become defensive; show compassion because the other person has been misled and misinformed. With gentleness and kindness, answer the criticism in order to correct false information, and then move ahead into further respectful, bridge-building conversation.

6. *Witness to Muslims individually.* Because of the shame culture, Muslims are sometimes afraid to ask questions about other faiths in front of other Muslims. They keep up a front of disinterest. So if I encounter a Muslim in a group and want to talk with him about Christ—even if he initiates with a question—I usually take him aside, one-on-one, or I set up an appointment to talk with him at another time. It's very important that your friend trusts you and feels open to talk about spiritual things and ask you questions that he or she cannot ask in front of other Muslims.

7. *Relax, don't panic.* All you have to do to swim on your back is to trust the water to lift you. You surrender the buoyancy of your body to the water. Likewise, whenever you're witnessing, you surrender and you trust God to give you wisdom in what to say and do. Pray that God will use you in your friend's life, and expect results. God will move in and through you to accomplish his will.

8. *Give a gift.* As we saw in chapter 3, gift giving solidifies relationships in a Middle Eastern culture. From the time Jesus was on earth, gift giving and blessing others has been a way to show love and respect. I recommend that you always have something to give to your Muslim friend—something spiritual in nature that focuses on the teachings of Jesus. For example, you could offer a Bible in his first language, or a New Testament in both English and Arabic. Many Muslims appreciate music; you might offer worship music in English or in his or her first language. If you're always prepared with this type of gift, you'll be continually providing your friend with more that has the potential to draw him closer to Christ.

BRIDGE BUILDING 101 SUMMARY

1. Always start by praying.

2. Ask for the Holy Spirit to fill your heart and mind.

3. Gather basic information.

4. Be straightforward.

5. Speak with a smile.

6. Witness to Muslims individually.

7. Relax, don't panic.

8. Give a gift.

You might be wondering if you have what it takes to be an ambassador. *Am I good enough to represent Christ to Muslims?* If your identity is in Christ, you are his ambassador. God has made you his representative, and that's the only qualification you need. Christians are not perfect, but they must be authentic. Be loving and friendly with your Muslim friends. Always point them away from you—the ambassador—and toward your leader, King Jesus.

> You might be wondering if you have what it takes to be an ambassador. *Am I good enough to represent Christ to Muslims?* If your identity is in Christ, you are his ambassador.

Closing prayer: *Heavenly Father, make me an ambassador for Christ. Use me to build bridges, not walls. May your love shine through me. In Christ's name! Amen.*

Part Two

"Always Be Prepared to Give an Answer"

Responding to Seven Common Questions Muslims Ask

It's Go Time

Did you know that more Muslims have become believers in Jesus in the past twenty years than in the preceding 1,400 years? The harvest is ripe! It's time to get involved in reaching Muslims and answering their most common questions. Most Muslims are not asking these questions simply to argue. No, most are genuinely curious. These questions alone demonstrate to us that they have been wrestling with their questions, maybe for years—and asking you, a follower of Jesus, to answer their questions takes an enormous amount of courage on their behalf. For a Muslim to ask a believer of Christ a legitimate question about the Christian faith means that the individual has reached a crucial point in his or her struggle to know the truth. We need to be people of compassion and people of prayer. We also must be prepared with answers to their questions. Scripture says, "But in your hearts revere Christ as Lord. Always be prepared to give an answer to everyone who asks you to give the reason for the hope that you have" (1 Peter 3:15).

The Bible compels us to be prepared with an answer, but this does not mean that you have it all together or that you are a spiritual superhero. To be prepared with an answer means that you, too, have struggled with similar questions and are willing to share what you understand about them. It means that you are willing to go the extra mile to help your Muslim friend find the answers he or she is looking for. Being prepared with an answer means that you are confident enough in your faith to be able to say, "I don't know exactly, but let's find out."

AN INFORMATION CRISIS

On a short-term trip to southern Spain, my group was giving out Arabic Bibles. I think one of the best ways to represent Jesus is to let people read his word, to let them hear what Jesus said. We set up a book table near the street curb. A car pulled up, and the driver peered out of his window to see what we were doing. His beard was bushy and grew down to his second button. I said to him, "*As-salaam alaikum.*" He replied, "*Alaikum salaam.*"

I said to him, "Sir, we are giving out the Injeel of the Messiah Jesus."

He raised his eyebrows and said to me, "I am the imam of Amsterdam. Have you read the Qur'an?"

I responded to him, "Yes, fourteen times."

He clarified, "In Arabic?"

Knowing where he was headed with his line of questioning, I said, "Of course, in Arabic. What, do I look French to you? I'm an Arab."

He shared with me, "I've read the Qur'an four times."

Even though I'm an evangelical minister, I had read the Qur'an more than this imam. I wanted to keep him engaged in our dialogue, so I asked him, "Well, have you read the Injeel of Jesus?" When he said he hadn't, I suggested to him, "You should read it so you can teach your people about what Jesus taught."

He considered his options and replied, "Since you've read the Qur'an, give me the Injeel and I'll read it." I passed him a copy and he went on his way.

As the imam pulled away from the curb, I experienced an intense personal struggle. The imam is a top religious leader for Muslims in Amsterdam (as he said). He is the one who is supposed to know what to teach his people. And he's never read the Injeel. So what could he possibly be teaching his people about Christians or about Jesus?

This is the crisis. Muslims don't know what we believe. They don't know that Jesus has come to be the Savior—*their* Savior. It is a crisis of information.

LIKE THE COINS IN YOUR POCKET

Coins are designed deliberately, right down to their size, edges and weight. This makes it possible to distinguish a penny from a nickel from a dime with your eyes closed. All pennies are designed to look and feel just like all other pennies. When I was growing up in the Christian faith, I thought that every evangelistic experience was going to look and feel like all the other ones. I thought that all of my witnessing experiences would look alike, just like pennies.

But I quickly discovered that witnessing is not like having a pile of pennies in my pocket. Every experience has its own feel. It's like having a collection of dimes and nickels and pennies. They're all American coins even though they each look and feel different from the others and have different values. But I know they're all American coins because they each have the words "In

God We Trust" and "Liberty" embossed on them in English. They also all feature American leaders and are minted with the words "United States of America" on the reverse side. The different coins have the same components to make them American.

It's the same with witnessing. Different evangelistic experiences will look different, but they share the core elements. Talking with a Shi'ite will look and feel different from talking with a Sunni, but the focal point of my witnessing will revolve around the gospel message, that Christ is the way, the truth and the life. Some witnessing opportunities might end with my friend asking for a Bible, or asking to pray to receive Christ, while other experiences will end with someone saying, "I don't want to talk to you." Regardless, my job is to be an ambassador, to make sure that I share the core truths about Jesus.

APPLYING BRIDGING SKILLS

Being asked by a Muslim to explain your faith is a privilege, and one that shouldn't be taken lightly. It is essential to apply the skills you have as an ambassador for Jesus: be loving and friendly toward them, aim to build a bridge, and remain biblical (see chapter 4 for the full discussion of ambassador qualities). As best as you can, endeavor to present Christ's gospel clearly through the questions Muslims ask. Establish a mood of truthfulness and openness with your Muslim friend so that the dialogue can continue and your friend feels respected, that his or her question is appreciated.

In Islam, asking tough questions about the Muslim faith is often considered undesirable. When faced with difficult questions, many imams reply, "Don't blaspheme against the Qur'an. Don't blaspheme against Allah." Muslims respect us more when we say to them, "I don't know, but let's study together," because in Islam, they don't have that option. When responded to respectfully, Muslims tend to realize, "My friend is at least honest.

He's not like my imam who gets upset if I ask questions."

It is important to remember that most children reared in a Christian home or society are raised to think for themselves. It's considered acceptable to go against the grain, even if everyone is against you. But in Muslim communities, the opposite is true. Your allegiance there is to the community, and the community is Muslim. Even if logic says Islam is wrong, your heart says to stick with Islam because it's important to stick with the community. This is why so many Muslims remain Muslim—it's a cultural decision, not a personal one. I once asked a friend, "Why don't you accept Christ as Savior?" He explained, "I agree with everything you're saying, but accepting Christ as Savior means I have to be against my culture and my family."

We must remain sensitive to our Muslim friends' culture and worldview. Pray for sincerity when witnessing to your Muslim friends. When they see you honestly seeking answers to their questions, you have the potential to ignite in them the search for truth.

These next chapters will present practical ways to respond to Muslims' commonly asked questions about Christianity by creating a bridge to understanding the message of Christ. We know that God has equipped us with the resources and biblical knowledge to respond honestly to tough questions about our faith. If you are a follower of Christ, you can have a gospel impact on Muslims.

Chapter 5

What Do You Think
of Muhammad?

Salvation is found in no one else,
for there is no other name under heaven given
to mankind by which we must be saved.

ACTS 4:12

MANY MUSLIMS ARE EAGER to know Christians' opinions about Muhammad, the final prophet in Islam. For Muslims, he is the model Muslim. He is someone they want to follow. It is natural for Muslims to be curious about what others think of him.

As committed followers of Jesus, we have no reason to feel intimidated by this challenging question. Our end goal is not to argue with our Muslim friends about Muhammad or Islam, but always to present the gospel clearly to them. By learning more about Muhammad's life, you will be in a position to build a bridge to the gospel and focus on common ideas with your Muslim friends.

HISTORICAL PERSPECTIVES

By the time Muhammad was born in A.D. 570, his father had

already passed away. There isn't much known about Muhammad's father, but we do know that his name was Abdullah, which is a Christian name. Meaning "servant of God," the name Abdullah was also one of the names of the apostle Paul, who would often say, "I am the servant of God." Christian Arabs used the name Abdullah to give glory to God.

At the time of Muhammad's birth, Arabian society was pagan and polytheistic. There were 360 gods in the Ka'aba that the Arabs would worship. Traveling caravans brought Arabs into contact with Christian and Jewish tribes. Muhammad was born into the Quraysh tribe, the highest tribe in Mecca. At the young age of six, Muhammad's mother died. He was raised by his grandfather for a time, then once his grandfather died, he was brought up by his uncle, Abu Talib. It's a rather sad story. He was an orphan, moved around from tent to tent, from family to family. You can imagine what kind of impact this irregular upbringing had on Muhammad. According to Islamic history, Muhammad was a sensitive young man who questioned why Arabs worshiped idols and did not worship one God like the Christians and the Jews.

At the age of twenty-five, Muhammad worked for a widow named Khadijah, who, according to historical tradition, was a Christian or part of a Christian cult. There is much dispute over her exact background. But because Muhammad was a faithful businessman, she proposed to him and they were married. Muhammad and Khadijah were married by her uncle, who is customarily understood to have been a Christian minister. Interestingly, this made their

Action Point

Read up on the history of Islam or the life of Muhammad. Read with the intention to become informed, not to become armed with ammunition.

marriage a Christian marriage. For as long as Muhammad and Khadijah were married, their relationship was between one husband and one wife. It was only after Khadijah's passing that Muhammad had multiple wives and concubines.

THE FIRST REVELATION AND THE QUR'AN

In A.D. 610, at the age of forty, Muhammad had his first revelation— that he was *al-rasul*, the messenger of Allah. At the time of this revelation, Muhammad had a high status in his society because he was married to Khadijah. Because of her wealth and prosperous business, he had the luxury of leisure time. The traditions of Islam uphold that he would go to a particular cave to meditate on God and religion. According to tradition, an angel appeared to Muhammad and told him to recite *"Ikra bismi rabikah aladhi khalak. Khalakah al-insana min alaq,"* which means, "Recite in the name of your God who created. [He] created man from a clot of blood." What Muhammad spoke became a part of the Qur'an.

Reportedly, Muhammad ran home to his wife to tell her of his encounter. Muhammad feared the visitation of this angel, whom he called Jibril (Gabriel in English). Khadijah eased his fears. Other family members also assuaged his worries and encouraged him to embrace the prophecy. Muhammad's first converts were his wife, Khadijah, close relatives Zaid and Ali, and his friends Abu Backer and Omar.

From the time of his revelation, Muhammad called for the worship of one God and stated that he himself was to be followed as the messenger of God. What Muhammad spoke became the Qur'an. It is important to understand that Islamic tradition reports that it was God who spoke to the angel Gabriel, who passed on God's word to Muhammad. Then Muhammad's followers would memorize it or write it on a piece of paper, leather or stone to be recorded later. It was the third successor of Muhammad who collected these words and compiled *Al Qur'an al Kareem*, the Holy Book of Islam.

MUHAMMAD IN MEDINA AND MECCA

In a journey known as the *Hijrah*, Muhammad left the city of Mecca for Medina in A.D. 622 as a result of persecution. This year marks the beginning of the Islamic calendar. In Medina, Muhammad became a popular political figure by uniting the tribes there. To be able to support themselves, Muhammad and his followers raided the passing caravans that were on their way to Mecca, which started a war between him and Quraish, the dominant tribe of Mecca. Muhammad won some battles, but lost others. Through a political ploy, he finally conquered Mecca in 630 and destroyed the idols of the Ka'aba. As more people were converted to Islam, they were compelled to speak Arabic, the language of the Qur'an.

Muhammad lived in Medina until his last pilgrimage to Mecca in 632, where he delivered his farewell address. The same year, he suddenly fell ill, died and was buried in Medina.

MUHAMMAD'S ACCOMPLISHMENTS

As you look at the life of Muhammad, you might find that you agree with certain actions he took. You might find that you question others. In any case, one of the most straightforward ways of answering your Muslim friend's question about what you think of Muhammad is to acknowledge some of his triumphs. This can actually be a great conduit to deepen the conversation with your friend.

> One of Muhammad's greatest accomplishments that we as Christians can agree with is that he taught the worship of one God.

One of Muhammad's greatest accomplishments that we as Christians can agree with is that he taught the worship of one

God. In Muhammad's time, Arab men were idolaters; they worshiped multiple gods. Muhammad and the Qur'an actually released the Arabs from paganism.

We also can point out that Muhammad stopped the practice of infanticide. In pre-Islamic Arabia, the practice of infanticide, especially female infanticide, was widespread among the pagans (idol worshipers). As a result of Muhammad's reforms, Islam forbids the practice of infanticide entirely, which is something that we as followers of Christ can find admirable.

> Focus on Muhammad's successes rather than his shortcomings. Your job as an ambassador is to move beyond the surface discussion about Muhammad into the real issue—they need a savior, and that Savior is Jesus.

Muhammad also gave more rights to women. Though we might observe that what rights he put forth were not many, in the Arab pagan community, women were afforded few rights at all. Muhammad taught that men and women are equal in the sight of God. This is a major improvement, and one that committed Christians can agree with. Finally, Muhammad abolished idols and destroyed them.

Action Point

Always move the discussion with a Muslim friend from Muhammad's strengths to the uniqueness of Jesus. You can share positive things about their religion while setting the stage to move the conversation to a much deeper level.

By focusing your view of Muhammad on his successes rather than his shortcomings, you can start to create bridges to Jesus, who also accomplished amazing feats. Your Muslim friends will respect that you see some positive aspects about their leader. This strategic

approach puts you in a position to share the ultimate triumph of
Jesus with them. Your job as an ambassador is to move beyond the
surface discussion about Muhammad into the real issue—they need
a savior, and that Savior is Jesus.

BRIDGING TO JESUS

When I start to create a bridge from Muhammad to Jesus, I try
to focus on the ideas that Jesus shared with his followers. I focus
on the person of Jesus and how I have a personal relationship
with him. This is such a radically different concept than what
Islam teaches. In Islam you follow the law. Muslims study the
law to obey. As believers in Christ, we study the Word to worship.
In Islam, God's word became a book. In Christianity, God's Word
became Jesus. See the difference? For followers of Jesus, he—not
a book—is the ultimate revelation of God.

I was speaking with a woman in Colorado who asked me what
I thought of Muhammad and Ali, the cousin of Muhammad. She
was struggling with her own beliefs. "I read the Qur'an," she said,
"and I know they were good people, but what do you think? I'm
attending a church and I'm interested in Christ and the Bible."

I started by sharing the good things that Muhammad did,
including that he gave more rights to
women. She was excited. "I know, I
know, they taught me that."

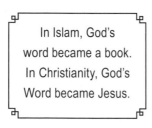

In Islam, God's
word became a book.
In Christianity, God's
Word became Jesus.

Seeing my opportunity to move our
dialogue to a deeper level, I explained,
"But the Bible says in Acts 4:12 that
there's only one Redeemer, Jesus Christ."

She agreed. "That's true. The Qur'an says Jesus is the intercessor
on the last day."

I continued, "Well, there are a lot of good people in the world,
but they're not going to save us. The only Savior is Jesus, and

that's why I am following Christ." As she listened intently, I persisted, "Jesus shows me that I have salvation, and I want to stick to Christ because he's the one who redeemed me."

That's what won her. Had I ranted about the negative side of Muhammad, I would have lost her. She already knew the negative side, and I knew it would be counterproductive to discuss his limitations. No one will tell you how inadequate their religion is.

There's no need to commit to agreeing that Muhammad was a prophet because we cannot say that. Islam teaches that God did not speak to Muhammad directly, but rather the angel Gabriel dictated the words of the Qur'an. Then other followers of Muhammad recorded what he said and collected it into the Qur'an. We have no way to verify what was recorded outside the Qur'an. So if I use the Qur'an at all, I point to where the Qur'an talks about Jesus. When we talk with Muslims about Jesus, we're not asking them to do anything wrong. Amazingly, the Qur'an mentions Jesus more than ninety times!

I'm careful to use discretion when referring to Muhammad as a prophet. Muhammad is never mentioned in the Bible, but I seek to remain respectful about their prophet by referring to him in an appropriate way. If I'm in the middle of a conversation with a Muslim, and he says about Muhammad, "Peace be upon him," I do not copy my friend and say the same thing. Instead, I would say, for example, "The messenger of Islam says this," or, "According to the prophet of Islam . . ." In this way, I define that he is the prophet of Islam, but that he is not my prophet.

Action Point

Decide in advance how you will refer to Muhammad in conversations with Muslims. In making your decision beforehand, you can focus on sharing the gospel message, rather than focusing on semantics.

However, it is helpful for Christians to realize that Muslims recognize many messengers. Throughout the centuries, God has sent many great men, and Muslims count Adam, Noah, Moses and Jesus among those prophets. For Muslims, Muhammad is simply the final messenger. The Qur'an even mentions John the Baptist, though it doesn't explain why he came.

These common links between the Qur'an and the Bible give us great opportunities to direct the conversation to the true Savior, provided we do so in love and with respect.

Can we fill in that gap for our Muslim friends? Of course! The only way to know why John the Baptist came is to read the Injeel. The Qur'an also declares that God sent Jonah. This is great news for us because Jonah preached the need for repentance. Can we talk about Jesus from the story of Jonah? Of course! These common links between the Qur'an and the Bible give us great opportunities to direct the conversation to the true Savior, provided we do so in love and with respect.

JESUS AND THE INJEEL

I was speaking at a hotel and my microphone was not working. So the woman in charge got on her walkie-talkie and requested, "Abdul, where are you? We need you." I lit up. "Abdul? Great! That's an Arabic name. Let's wait for Abdul." When Abdul showed up, I found out that he was from Morocco.

"*As-salaam alaikum*," I greeted him.

"*Alaikum salaam*," he responded. "So what are you speaking about?"

I replied, "I'm speaking on how to build bridges between Islam and Christianity and about how Muslims and Christians can develop better relationships."

He nodded his head and said, "Yes, we are from the same religion."

I thought to myself, *I don't know how that is,* but that's what he said. Seeing an opportunity to witness to Abdul, I said to him, "The Lord Jesus said to love your neighbor as yourself."

He responded in turn, "The prophet Muhammad said the same thing."

Surprised, I asked, "Prophet Muhammad said the same thing?"

He explained, "Yes, the prophet Muhammad said if you buy a leg of lamb and your neighbor is too poor to have meat, wrap the lamb with paper so your neighbor won't see it and get jealous." He concluded, "It's the same idea as what you said."

My role is not to criticize Islam or Muhammad. But I did see that I needed to move the conversation in a different direction, so I said to him, "That's interesting. You know, the Messiah Jesus said, 'Love your enemies.'"

Action Point

Seek out the little opportunities to meet Muslims. They all need Jesus.

Now it was his turn to be surprised. "Prophet *Issa* said, 'Love your enemies'?" he questioned.

I opened the Injeel to Matthew 26:32, where Jesus says, "Put your sword back. . . . All who draw the sword will die by the sword."

Intrigued, Abdul leaned in to read the verse in Arabic. Then he looked up and asked, "Can I keep this Injeel?" Abdul had been in America for six years. I didn't do anything except show him a verse in Arabic, and he wanted to read more. Let's say he took the Injeel home, but he didn't read it; instead, his wife read it. Maybe his sister read it. The most important thing is to give Muslims access to the New Testament. We can trust that Jesus will reveal himself to them in his way and in his time.

One of the most prominent differences between Jesus and Muhammad is that Muhammad gave his followers laws, whereas Jesus gave his followers principles to live by. It is said that Muhammad grew his beard without trimming it, and that he supposedly entered the tub with his right foot first when he bathed. Therefore, "good" Muslims who want to follow Muhammad will also grow beards in the same way and enter the bath the same way. Muslims are taught to follow an example, to follow the rules.

But Jesus did not give us laws to follow; he gave us principles to live by. "Love your neighbor as yourself," he said (Matthew 22:39). I can do this anywhere. I can

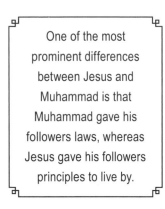

> One of the most prominent differences between Jesus and Muhammad is that Muhammad gave his followers laws, whereas Jesus gave his followers principles to live by.

"love my neighbor" in Lebanon, in Syria, in Cyprus, in Africa, in America. I can love my neighbor next door, at the grocery store, at the coffee shop or in a parking lot. It's a principle to live by. As another example, Jesus says, "A man will leave his father and mother and be united to his wife, and the two will become one flesh" (Matthew 19:5). This is a principle. Jesus doesn't tell us how we become one; instead, we are to live out oneness. We can communicate these principles with our Muslim friends as a way to spur conversations to share the gospel message with them. Our goal is to show that the Injeel clearly states that Christ alone is the Intercessor and that humanity's salvation was provided by Jesus the Redeemer. Jesus—not Muhammad—is the Savior from sin.

Action Point

In conversations with Muslims, aim to show that Jesus is the Redeemer, the Savior from sin.

As we invite our Muslim friends to explore the Injeel, we pray that they, too, will find that there is only one God and one Mediator, Christ the Messiah, Jesus, who was born of the Virgin Mary. As committed believers we love and respect all people, but Christ is the only Redeemer. He said that anyone who commits sin is a slave of sin, but if Jesus sets you free, you are free indeed (John 8:34-36). Let's continue to endeavor to reach our Muslim friends so that they can experience Christ's freedom.

Closing prayer: *Heavenly Father, thank you for your love to all nations. Thank you that you can save all people. You alone are holy! May I trust your sovereign hand as I point Muslims to follow Jesus. In Christ's name, amen.*

Chapter 6

Hasn't the Injeel
Been Corrupted?

All Scripture is God-breathed and is useful for teaching,
rebuking, correcting and training in righteousness,
so that the servant of God may be thoroughly
equipped for every good work.

2 TIMOTHY 3:16-17

—•—

THOUGH MUSLIMS CLAIM that the Injeel has been corrupted, most have never read it for themselves. As a case in point, I was talking to my friend Kamal, a Shi'ite Muslim. I asked him, "Kamal, have you read the Injeel?"

He scoffed, "No, it's been changed."

I countered, "Well, if you haven't read it, how do you know it's been changed?"

He replied, "Well, my dad told me it was."

I asked him, "Did your dad read the Injeel?"

"No," Kamal responded.

"So how does he know it's been changed?" I urged.

"Well," said Kamal, "Grandpa told him it was."

I couldn't help but ask, "Did Grandpa read the Injeel?" And of course, Kamal replied that his grandfather hadn't read the Injeel. Misinformation is being passed down through generations.

Action Point

Find out from your Muslim friends if they have read the Injeel, or if anyone in their family has read the Injeel.

When witnessing to Muslims, we must cut to the heart of the matter: the Bible is trustworthy and should be followed. Our goal is not to convert Muslims—for who can convert anyone's heart except God?—but is instead to encourage and invite our Muslim friends to read the Injeel. Using conversational apologetics, we want to lift the veil of misunderstanding concerning the Injeel so that Muslims will read it for themselves.

THE LOGIC BEHIND THE QUESTION

At my office, we had a problem with our computer system, so we called in a computer expert. I found out he was an atheist, but I was curious if he had read the Bible at all. He scorned, "It has 1,001 mistakes." One thousand and one mistakes! I handed him my business card, saying, "Will you please email me the mistakes?" That exchange happened years ago, and I'm still waiting for him to send me the mistakes.

Using conversational apologetics, we want to lift the veil of misunderstanding concerning the Injeel so that Muslims will read it for themselves.

The accusation that the Bible has been changed is parroted around the world by many people, whether religious or agnostic. They refuse to accept Christ's teachings because they claim that the text was corrupted in the process of copying it. Therefore, they say, God sent other messengers and teachers to provide the true message.

When Muslims bring up the argument that the Injeel has been corrupted, typically they are indicating that the Injeel has gone through many versions and the real message has been lost. Some imams also teach that Christians have changed and added stories and erased any references to Islam and Muhammad. However, this view is not backed up by research.

Muslims tend to reason that the *Tawrat* (Torah) of Moses was corrupted, so God sent the *Zabur* (Psalms). However, the Zabur became corrupted, and so God sent the Injeel. But because the Injeel became corrupted, God had to send the Qur'an. Contradictorily, Muslims believe that the Qur'an will never be changed, since God keeps and protects his Word.

THE ZERO-CORRUPTION BRIDGE

To explain in detail to Muslims how the Injeel has not been corrupted, I encourage you to use the zero-corruption bridge approach, which examines the development of the Injeel from theological, logical and historical points of view.

Theological considerations. When Muslims say that the Bible has been corrupted, we can respond with the phrase "*Astaghfur 'allah!*" which asks for God to forgive the person for his blasphemy. If humans are able to corrupt the Word of God, then this also means that humans are stronger and keener than God, and we know this to be impossible.

As followers of Jesus Christ, we believe that God exists and that he is both a powerful and communicative God. His love for mankind compels him to communicate his truths. Therefore, we find that the Injeel is inspired and protected by God and that it is historically authentic.

We can respond to Muslims' claims about the corruption of the Injeel by explaining that God inspired the writing of the Injeel and that God's Word cannot be changed by humans. God will keep his Word as he promised in the Injeel itself (Mark 13:31), and his Word will be used to enlighten and judge the human race.

> God will keep his Word as he promised in the Injeel itself (Mark 13:31), and his Word will be used to enlighten and judge the human race.

Logical considerations. Though many Muslims are adamant that the Injeel has been corrupted, those I have spoken with cannot provide any evidence to that effect. Looking objectively at whether or not the Injeel has been corrupted, these questions must be answered:

- Who corrupted the Injeel?
- When was the Injeel corrupted?
- Where was the Injeel corrupted?
- Why was the Injeel corrupted?
- Where is the original Injeel?
- What parts of the Injeel were corrupted?
- Was the Injeel corrupted before or after the life of Muhammad?

Action Point

Be prepared with questions you can ask your Muslim friend about the corruption of the Injeel.

Christians, Muslims, Hindus and others are all searching for the truth. We are all pilgrims on a journey to know the truth about God and his will for our lives. Sincere seekers of truth will discover that there is no answer to these questions because the Injeel is authenticated by history.

Historical considerations. When I witness to Muslims about the integrity of the Injeel, I like to begin by asking them if I can share my historical research with them. I find that this sets a tone of respect and helps them to see that I am not just sharing my personal opinion, but that I am basing my explanation on verifiable facts.

When I use this approach, 90 percent of the time I hear from my friend, "Can I have a copy of the Injeel?" Praise God! His request means I got through to him! We can trust that the Bible is mightier than a double-edged sword and that as our Muslim friends begin to explore the Injeel, God will speak to them personally and will reveal himself to them.

I try to keep the explanation of the historical development of the Injeel straightforward by focusing on three different stages: the eyewitness stage (A.D. 1–100), the persecution stage (A.D. 100–325) and the translation stage (A.D. 325–present).

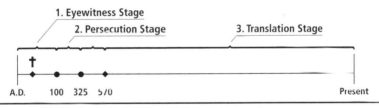

Figure 6.1: Timeline from A.D. to present (*Bridges* booklet, p. 33).

THE EYEWITNESS STAGE

When we speak of the eyewitness stage, we are referring to the years A.D. 1–100. In A.D. 33, Jesus Christ of Nazareth was crucified and raised from the dead. By A.D. 100, most of the books of the New Testament were written (on papyri in Koine Greek, lingua franca of the Roman Empire), and there were no living eyewitnesses of the life, crucifixion and resurrection of Christ. Until then, while eyewitnesses were still living, any misrepresentation of Jesus' teachings would have been rejected because they knew the truth. At the same time, if the followers of Christ transcribed his words incorrectly from the beginning, the Injeel and the Christian faith would never have existed.

In addition to these eyewitnesses' being alive and attesting to the truth of the Injeel's message, two other realities contribute to the Injeel's trustworthiness. First, people tend to lie for personal gain or to cover up a shameful situation. However, many followers of Jesus died claiming that Jesus is the Messiah who died and rose again. Second, no conclusive evidence was available to show that Jesus was in the grave. The eyewitnesses who were opposed to Christ could have brought his body forward as proof that the resurrection did not happen.

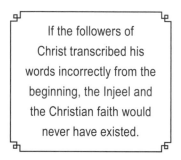

If the followers of Christ transcribed his words incorrectly from the beginning, the Injeel and the Christian faith would never have existed.

Only after the last eyewitness died around A.D. 100 would the first opportunity arise to corrupt the Word of God.

THE PERSECUTION STAGE

I refer to the years between the eyewitness stage and the translation stage as the persecution stage. During these 225 years, Christians everywhere were persecuted and killed in gruesome ways. The Jewish leaders harassed and killed them. The Romans considered them atheists because they did not believe in a pantheon of gods. Considering Christians to be a great threat, the Romans scared others from joining the Christian faith by ordering them to be killed and burned, along with their books.

Even in the age of persecution against Jesus' followers, it is highly unlikely that the Injeel became corrupted. Four evidences prove that the Injeel's integrity was preserved:

- Partial manuscripts
- Church fathers
- Lectionaries
- Early translations

Partial manuscripts. Borrowing from the Egyptians, the books of the New Testament were copied by hand on manuscripts made of papyri. As the manuscripts slowly deteriorated over time, early Christians started copying the books of the Injeel as new churches were established.

Most members of the Christian community couldn't afford a personal copy of the entire Injeel. So, partial manuscripts—a few books of the New Testament, but not the entire text—were produced and distributed among Christian believers. Depending on the size of the Christian community, more copies were available. Archaeologists have found 13,000 manuscripts that date between the years A.D. 100 and 325. They are all written in Koine Greek and include the whole books of the Injeel, accounts of the cruci fixion and resurrection of Christ, and records of the uniqueness of Jesus and his atoning death and resurrection. These manuscripts are in complete harmony with latter manuscripts.

Moreover, comparing these partial manuscripts to one other establishes the manuscripts' consistency and shows that they were all copied from the same original source. Though these manuscripts were copied around the Mediterranean Sea and dis-

Action Point

Brush up on your history to be able to provide your Muslim friend with a brief historical overview of the reliability of the Injeel. Commit to memory some important dates and events. More in-depth study is found in my book *Is the Injeel Corrupted?* (fouadmasri.com).

tributed to different areas and regions, they all agree with one another and with the later codices.

Church fathers. As further proof, "church fathers," who were the immediate disciples of the disciples of Christ, wrote letters to one another on matters of theology and the Christian life. They quoted from the copies of the New Testament they each had in their possession. These quotations from the Injeel are in direct agreement with the partial manuscripts and later manuscripts. Because the later manuscripts agree with the partial manuscripts and letters from the church fathers, there is no doubt that the New Testament was transmitted without fault or change.

Lectionaries. The existence of church lectionaries is one of the most important evidences of the Injeel's credibility. Lectionaries contained the appointed readings (or "lections") for each day of the church year. As such, they were extremely important to individual churches. Since many Christians did not own a personal copy of the New Testament, they depended on these service books for learning and growing in knowledge of God's Word.

The number of known lectionaries has jumped to about 2,300 copies. In addition, almost 3,200 continuous-text manuscripts exist, bearing witness to the widespread and widely read nature of the Injeel during this time frame between A.D. 100 and 325.

Early translations. Complete manuscripts of the Injeel translated from Greek to other Mediterranean languages are important in verifying the New Testament's reliability. One such copy in Syriac is known as the Peshitto. Translations such as this can be reverse translated to check their reliability with the original Greek manuscripts.

THE TRANSLATION STAGE

The Injeel was faithfully copied and distributed as Christianity spread throughout Africa, Europe and Asia. As the Injeel was reproduced into different languages, translators were meticulous in keeping each copy consistent with the manuscripts available to them.

A precious, handwritten copy of the New Testament, the Codex Sinaiticus, was found in Saint Catherine's Monastery on Mount Sinai and is dated to A.D. 325. From this manuscript, other Bible versions are translated. Other codices, including the Codex Vaticanus (dated A.D. 350) and the Codex Alexandrinus (dated

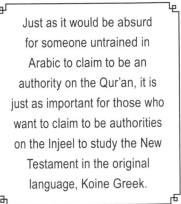

Just as it would be absurd for someone untrained in Arabic to claim to be an authority on the Qur'an, it is just as important for those who want to claim to be authorities on the Injeel to study the New Testament in the original language, Koine Greek.

A.D. 400), contain the most complete manuscripts of the New Testament. All present-day translations go back to the Greek manuscripts. The message is one and the meaning is the same. The different "versions" that Muslims claim exist are merely translations. Just as it would be absurd for someone untrained in Arabic to claim to be an authority on the Qur'an, it is just as important for those who want to claim to be authorities on the Injeel to study the New Testament in the original language, Koine Greek.

The dating of these manuscripts is significant. Muhammad was born in A.D. 570. Because he commanded the reading of the Injeel as part of Islam, we know that the manuscripts predated Muhammad, that the manu-

Action Point

Consider reading the writings of F. F. Bruce and Josh McDowell to learn more about this subject. However, the information presented here is sufficient to communicate the reliability of the Injeel to your friend.

scripts were in existence and that they were considered reliable.

A careful examination of Christian history from the death and resurrection of Christ to the present day reveals a thread of faithfulness to the preservation of God's revealed Word.

THE INJEEL SPEAKS FOR ITSELF

Nadia, a follower of Christ, was having a conversation with her friend Huda, a devout Sunni Muslim woman. The Muslim woman asked Nadia, "What do you do when you have problems with your family?"

Nadia replied simply, "I pray."

Confused, Huda rejoined, "No, you don't really pray."

With equal confusion Nadia replied, "No, I do pray."

The two women went back and forth on this issue until Huda explained, "I've never seen you bow down toward Rome." In Islam, Muslims bow toward Mecca during times of prayer, so Huda thought that Christians pray by bowing toward another city.

Finally understanding Huda's bewilderment, Nadia clarified, "The Bible shows that we can pray anytime, anywhere, because the whole planet is a temple of worship to God."

Huda was so intrigued that she asked for an Injeel. Two years later, this devout Muslim woman was baptized. At her baptism, Huda shared, "I read the Injeel and I found the friend who will never leave me, because Jesus says, 'I will never leave you, nor forsake you.'"

> We must trust that the Injeel can and will speak for itself, for "the word of God is alive and active" (Hebrews 4:12).

The beauty of this story is that the Lord worked in Huda's heart through his Word and through the prayers of Nadia. Nadia didn't disparage Muhammad or malign Islam. She was just being like Jesus, having a spirit of compassion and a spirit of prayer. We must trust that the Injeel can and will speak for itself, for "the word of God is alive and active" (Hebrews 4:12). We can have confidence that the Injeel is reliable and trustworthy and that the Lord will use it to speak to our Muslim friends.

When we witness to our Muslim friends either by using the Injeel or speaking about the integrity of the Injeel, we seek to remain loving and friendly, to have a bridging approach, and to be biblical. One way to straightforwardly explain the reliability of the Injeel is to be prepared with a streamlined explanation that sums up the main points:

- As believers in God, we refuse to accept that any human can corrupt the Injeel.

- Moses, David and Jesus were sent to a people who believed in God.

- Muhammad's generation was pagan and needed to worship one God, and this lesson was taught to the Jewish people from the days of Abraham (Arabic: *Ibrahim*).

- Although Muhammad and the Qur'an came last chronologically, the core message had been revealed from the days of Abraham.

- Unlike the Qur'an, the Injeel moves beyond monotheism to deal with issues of salvation, grace, faith, sanctification and holiness.

- Christians can agree with what the Qur'an says when it agrees with the Injeel. However, the teachings of the Qur'an must correspond with the Injeel to be accepted.

- To understand more fully the will of God for their life, it is essential for Muslims to study the entire Bible.

Action Point

Always keep in mind how you can demonstrate the attitudes of an ambassador of Jesus (see chapter 4).

Should you have an opportunity to discuss the development and trustworthiness of the Injeel at deeper levels, you can have confidence that the more detailed explanations of how the Injeel was not corrupted will prove helpful in talking with your Muslim friends.

The beauty of the Injeel is that it allows us to read all literature about God and then examine it in light of the Injeel. Even the Old Testament is to be read in the light of the New Testament! We know that Jesus is the ultimate revelation: "In the past God spoke to our ancestors through the prophets at many times and in various ways, but in these last days he has spoken to us by his Son" (Hebrews 1:1-2). It is impossible to understand God's revelation without Jesus' words. Not all religions say this!

Jesus also said, "You did not choose me, but I chose you and appointed you so that you might go and bear fruit—fruit that will last" (John 15:16). This is an amazing privilege. Jesus entrusts us with a beautiful message to tell our neighbors, our enemies—anybody!—that he has salvation waiting for them.

So when I conclude a discussion with someone about the authenticity of the Injeel, I don't stop there. I ask them, "Since the Bible was not changed, would you like to receive Christ?" My friend might say, "I need some time to think." Should I give him the time to think? Yes, of course! It is not our job to push the issue. We are ambassadors—we offer invitations, not force decisions.

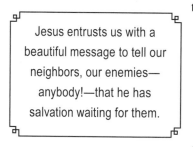

Jesus entrusts us with a beautiful message to tell our neighbors, our enemies—anybody!—that he has salvation waiting for them.

But I will say that 99 percent of the times that I ask my friends if they would like to receive Christ, I hear from them, "Can I have a Bible?" Praise God! For when my friend asks for a Bible, it is a sign that I really got through to him. The true Word of God is not the text; the true Word of God is Jesus. The reason we respect the text is because it is about Jesus, and it is Jesus who will speak to my Muslim friend.

A while ago, I was conducting a training program for Arabs on how to witness to Muslims. I asked Abdul how he became a follower of Christ, and he shared his story with me. "I was listening to a Christian radio station from Europe. My father, who is a Muslim judge, saw me and asked what I was trying to do. I explained to him, 'I'm trying to get a station.' My father was more discerning and asked, 'Are you trying to get those Christian stations?' I admitted that I was. 'Come to my office' he said."

Abdul's father told him, "Your brother, twenty years ago, wrote to one of those stations and they sent him an Injeel. I hid the Injeel in this drawer, but I'll give it to you and you can read it and see that this religion is false."

Action Point

Be bold and offer your Muslim friend an invitation to receive Christ, or at least to receive a copy of the Injeel to read on their own. Part of our responsibility as ambassadors is to equip our new friends with resources that can help them draw near to God.

The father unlocked the drawer and took out a copy of the book of John. Abdul started reading it, and in one year he prayed to receive Christ. Today Abdul is serving God in Africa. I find that this story has profound implications. The Word of God was hidden there in Abdul's home for twenty years, but when it came out, his soul was won. The Injeel speaks for itself.

We must remember that the goal in sharing about the Injeel is not the historical proof. We offer historical evidence to get a listening ear. What will truly win over our Muslim friends is the love of Christ.

> What will truly win over our Muslim friends is the love of Christ.

Closing prayer: *Our Heavenly Father, thank you for revealing yourself throughout history. You are the Almighty and no one is stronger than you. Thank you for protecting the Bible for our guidance. May I always share your precious message to all humanity. In Jesus' name, amen.*

Chapter 7

Who Is Jesus, the Son of Mary?

She will give birth to a son, and you are to give him the name
Jesus, because he will save his people from their sins.

MATTHEW 1:21

—•—

WHILE TALKING TO MY FRIEND HASSAN in the Middle East,
he shared with me, "I was raised to see that Islam is superior to
Christianity, but as I studied the life of Jesus in the Injeel, Jesus
showed me that he is much more than what I believed. I could
not resist that. I could not resist the power of who Jesus is." It
wasn't long before my friend came to faith in Christ.

The power of Christ cannot be denied. He offers grace. He
changes hearts. He sees where we are and he still offers his love.
He shepherds us back to him because of his amazing love for us.
Growing up, in my home city of Beirut I never saw an actual
shepherd. But I spent my summers away from the city, in the
mountains, where it is much cooler. It was there that I finally
learned what shepherding really looks like.

We had a neighbor in the mountains who was a shepherd.
While talking to him one day, I noticed that the sheep were

rather stupid animals. When they were sent into the fields, they couldn't find their way back home. My neighbor said, "I always have to make sure I can see where the sheep are, because if the shepherd is not there, they are in a crisis."

Jesus saw human history, saw how we start wars with one another and kill one another, and still he chose to shower his love and kindness on us. Matthew 9:36 reads, "When he saw the crowds, he had compassion on them, because they were harassed and helpless, like sheep without a shepherd." Many people are in a crisis today, outside of a relationship with Jesus, the Shepherd.

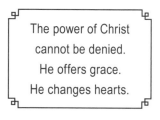

The power of Christ cannot be denied. He offers grace. He changes hearts.

WHERE IS THE GOOD NEWS?

Christ himself was born in Bethlehem at a time filled with violence and strife. Sin will always have the same symptoms and will always be the reason behind murdering, stealing, lying, cheating, dishonoring and oppressing others. The good news is that a Savior, the Messiah, was born into this world. Christ the Redeemer was born to a virgin, lived a perfect life, died and rose again for the salvation of all nations.

However, today as we look at the Middle East, we do not see good news. There are wars, rumors of wars, news of oppression, violence and people dying for their faith and their allegiance to Christ. What shall we do with the information and news from Syria, Egypt, Afghanistan, Pakistan and North Africa? Are we to go into

Action Point

Keep up on current events in the Muslim world. You might find a topic to discuss with a Muslim that could lead to deeper conversations.

hiding? Are we to think on the evil and sin and forget what God has done? No, we cannot. We have a hope that must be shared with those who are lost.

We must not be afraid to share the joy that we have found with our Muslim friends. For "the angel said to them, 'Do not be afraid. I bring you good news that will cause great joy for all the people. Today in the town of David a Savior has been born to you; he is the Messiah, the Lord. This will be a sign to you: You will find a baby wrapped in cloths and lying in a manger'" (Luke 2:10-12). Jesus is the good news. We must be like the shepherds and angels and go tell Muslims the good news that a Savior has been born and will save us all from sin and lead us to eternal life!

Misconceptions About Jesus

We must remember that most Muslims are nominal Muslims—they have studied neither the Qur'an nor the Bible. They tend to make their own understanding of religion from hearsay or tradition. Over time, truths about Jesus become twisted or distorted. As believers in Christ, it is our responsibility to help our Muslim friends have an accurate understanding of who Jesus is. We must be able to give a clear explanation of Jesus' incarnation and identity as the Word of God.

One of the most common erroneous beliefs Muslims have about Christianity relates to the concept of Jesus as the Son of God. In the Bible, Jesus is called the Son of God, which makes Muslims accuse us of teaching that Jesus was half human, half divine. Many think that Christians teach that God had a physical relationship with Mary—specifically, that God incarnated in Gabriel and had sexual relations with Mary. The offspring is called the Son of God, which is blasphemy in Islam. This would make Jesus like the Greek mythological character Hercules.

Muslims find this detestable because Jesus is a prophet of

Islam. Jesus in Islam is just a man—he was a *rasul*, a messenger. The struggle today is that Jesus in the Injeel is different from the Jesus in Islam. Our real hurdle here is to help our Muslim friends see that Jesus in Islam is incorrect. Muslims need to go back to the Injeel to learn more about who Jesus is, because how Jesus is understood in Islam is not how Jesus is presented in the Injeel.

To gain a more precise understanding of Jesus, Muslims also need to read the Injeel to discover who Jesus is and what Jesus came to teach. Jesus was much more than a man—indeed, he is the Word of God. Since he is the Word of God, he is equal with God and has the same power of God. Jesus, Son of God, is a miracle of God—not a product of God's having a sexual relationship with Mary.

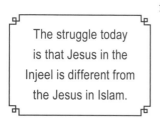

> The struggle today is that Jesus in the Injeel is different from the Jesus in Islam.

To Muslims, the term "Son of God" means something radically different than what it means to a follower of Christ. For us, Jesus in the Bible is the Word of God become flesh. He is the Son of God because God performed the miracle of creating Jesus, and we want to give glory to God. The sonship of Christ in the Bible is a *spiritual* sonship. Jesus said God is spirit. He is not flesh—he's an entirely different dimension. God is spirit, and so the sonship relationship is one that is spiritual.

When I was at a mosque one time, an engineer was speaking about Jesus. He proclaimed, "If you say that Jesus is the son of God, meaning that he is the best representation of God and the closest to God, Muslims agree." He continued, "If you say that Jesus is the son of God as a result of sexual relations

Action Point

Don't hesitate to offer your Muslim friends opportunities to receive their own copies of the Injeel.

between God and Mary, Muslims disagree."

I was completely baffled. Where in Christianity is it taught that God had a sexual relationship with Mary? Nowhere! This thought is offensive to all Christians. Muslims are purporting this idea to make the waters murky, to attract followers to Islam by saying that Christians and Muslims agree there was a miracle, that there was a virgin birth and that Jesus was a unique person.

Action Point

It is entirely intriguing that Jesus is mentioned more than ninety times in the Qur'an, and he is mentioned as the word of God. The Qur'an elevates Jesus and respects Muhammad. However, Islamic leaders will teach that Jesus is respected, but that Muhammad is elevated. The struggle we have—and the joy we have—is to help our Muslim friends understand that Jesus was much more than just a man. We must use what the Injeel teaches directly about Jesus to clarify the misunderstandings and the misinformation they have about Jesus.

Think about reading either the Qur'an as a whole or reading up on where Jesus is mentioned in the Qur'an. You'll have a better understanding of your Muslim friend's position, and your friend will be intrigued that you took the time to read his or her religion's holy book.

Bridging Between the Qur'an and the Injeel

The best way to know about a leader is to read his book. The best way to know more about Muhammad is to read the Qur'an, and the best way to know more about Jesus is to read the Injeel. This is where we come in. God can use you and me to start with Jesus in the Qur'an or Jesus in Islam by saying, "Oh, great! You believe all this about him, and that's wonderful. But you're missing the point that Jesus controlled the wind and the sea, and that Jesus raised the dead. That Jesus rose himself from the dead. That Jesus forgives our sins." These are not easy hurdles to cross, but we find our joy in seeing how God uses us to bring and explain these truths to our Muslim friends.

It is to our advantage that we can agree with many ideas about Jesus that come from the Qur'an. We have already seen that the Qur'an teaches that Jesus is the word of God (*Kalimat Allah*) (Qur'an 4:171). Praise God! We can concur with our Muslim friends that there is no difference between God and his Word. Muslims believe that Jesus was born of the virgin and conceived by the power of the Holy Spirit. Moreover, Muslims believe that Jesus was pure and sinless from birth, that he raised the dead and healed the sick, that he is coming back to earth, and that he will be a judge on Judgment Day. The Qur'an sets us up to be able to start a discussion with our Muslim friends about Jesus by *agreeing* with them on several points. From there, we can begin to elaborate on the truths about Jesus from the Injeel.

> It is to our advantage that we can agree with many ideas about Jesus that come from the Qur'an.

Jesus as the Word of God. One of the first misunderstandings to clarify is that Jesus is the Son of God because he is the Word of God become man. John 1:1-4 describes, "In the beginning was the Word, and the Word was with God, and the Word was God. He was with God in the beginning. Through him all things were made; without him nothing was made that has been made. In him was life, and that life was the light of all mankind." The Word of God became Jesus, and there

Action Point

Be aware of where the Qur'an and Injeel intersect to be able to bridge conversations easily. See resources at fouadmasri.com.

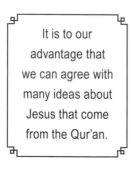

is no difference between God and his Word.

No separation. Many Muslims understand that Allah's word and Allah are the same. For us, this is a great bridge because the Bible calls Jesus the Son of God. God's Word became flesh, and that's why Christ is called the Son of God. That's why we respect Jesus and why we worship Jesus. We know that he is above any other prophet because he is the Word of God become flesh. There's no separation between God and his Word, for whatever God can do, his Word can do.

As both the Word of God and the Son of God, Jesus becomes the best representation of God and his plan for us. In Jesus' being the Word of God made flesh, glory is given to both Jesus' divinity and to God's miraculous power.

The many names of Jesus. Beyond "the Word of God," Jesus is also known by many names—the Good Shepherd; the Way, the Truth and the Life; the Resurrection; the Bread of Heaven; the Water of Life; the Conqueror; the Redeemer. All of these titles explain how Jesus Christ of Nazareth came to fulfill prophecy two thousand years ago by becoming the incarnate Word of God. Sharing with Muslims the names and titles of the Messiah Jesus helps them see the uniqueness and power of Christ.

The incarnation of God in Jesus Christ. As humans, we have limited understanding of the incarnation, which means how God can become man. This was a tremendous miracle that cannot be fully comprehended or explained. In 1 Timothy 3:16, the Injeel captures the mystery shrouding the incarnation:

> Beyond all question, the mystery from which true godliness springs is great:
>
> He appeared in the flesh,
>> was vindicated by the Spirit,
> was seen by angels,
>> was preached among the nations,

was believed on in the world,
was taken up in glory.

Christ as the greatest. In the story of the transfiguration, we know that Jesus took Peter, James and John up to a high mountain, and that Moses and Elijah appeared. Yet God showed the disciples that Jesus is greater than Elijah and greater than Moses, that he was pleased with Jesus. It is important for our Muslim friends to understand that the Injeel clearly shows that Christ is greater than anyone else. Jesus is greater than all the prophets. He is the Son of God, born of a virgin. He is the Word of God made flesh. He is the hope of the world.

> Jesus is greater than all the prophets. He is the Son of God, born of a virgin. He is the Word of God made flesh. He is the hope of the world.

The Messiah answers prayer. On a bus trip from Beirut to Damascus, our bus driver kept stopping at gas stations along the way. I finally had to ask him, "Sir, why do you keep stopping every few minutes? We need to get to the border."

He explained, "My tire is low on air. And it's Friday. I'm afraid they will close early, and I need an air pump to pump my tire."

Seizing the opportunity to witness to him, I asked our bus driver, "We are all here believers in Jesus. Can we pray that God helps us find a gas station that has an air pump?"

The look on the driver's face was priceless. Skeptically, he answered slowly, "Okay, you can pray." We prayed for our driver to be able to find a gas station with the air pump he needed. Within minutes he saw a gas station and pulled over. Praise God! There was an air pump!

Astounded, our driver looked at me with wide eyes. "Oh, Messiah Jesus answers prayer!" he exclaimed. When we reached our destination and said our goodbyes, the driver asked us for a copy of the Injeel. Did God care about his need? Of course! And having had an encounter with God, this man was no longer just looking for somebody to pump the air; he was looking for a Savior. Our new friend was being set free.

The way to salvation. Christ came as the Savior to save people from their sin. Jesus said, "So if the Son sets you free, you will be free indeed" (John 8:36). Isn't that refreshing? Jesus sets us free! As the Word of God and the Son of God, Jesus is the only One who can set people free.

We must introduce this path to freedom to our friends from Muslim backgrounds. Only through Christ can they understand God, have a way to God and experience true salvation.

Closing prayer: *Our heavenly Father, thank you for the Messiah Jesus. Thank you for his life, teaching and salvation. Empower me to share the Messiah with my Muslim friends. In Christ's name, amen.*

Chapter 8

Who Actually Died on the Cross?

I want to know Christ—yes, to know the power of his resurrection and participation in his sufferings, becoming like him in his death.

PHILIPPIANS 3:10

—•—

WHAT GLORIFIES GOD MORE?

On one of our summer trips to Lebanon, our team went to downtown Beirut to find some authentic baklava. In America we only have a few types of baklava, but in Lebanon we have thirty-plus types. As we drifted into a baklava shop, the smell of sugar made our mouths water. After enjoying our delicious dessert, I approached the counter to take care of the check.

The owner greeted me, "*As-salaam alaikum.*" I replied, "*Alaikum salaam.* Sir, I'd like to pay our bill."

He gave me the once-over and asked, "Are you evangelical?" I was floored. I don't know how he guessed.

I responded, "Yes, sir, we're all evangelicals, and we're here to pray for God to bless Beirut and to bless Lebanon."

Without skipping a beat, he objected, "Evangelicals are wrong."

A little taken aback, I repeated his statement back to him,

asking, "Evangelicals are wrong?" He started to explain what he meant.

"Yes, because the Injeel has been changed. The New Testament has been corrupted. The Bible is wrong because it says that Jesus died on the cross."

Taking a moment to gather my thoughts, I finally asked him, "What do you think glorifies God more? To help Jesus run away or to help Jesus conquer death?"

Surprised by my question, he asked me to repeat it. I reiterated, "What would glorify God more? To help Jesus escape death, or to allow Jesus to die and to raise him from the dead, therefore fulfilling the prophecy that Jesus would die and be raised from the dead?"

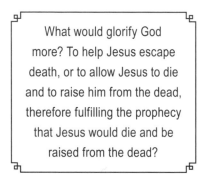

What would glorify God more? To help Jesus escape death, or to allow Jesus to die and to raise him from the dead, therefore fulfilling the prophecy that Jesus would die and be raised from the dead?

Not having an answer to my question, he tried to gloss over the issue. "Well, there are other things around us that glorify God," he explained.

I responded, "Yes, but Jesus is the only one who died and rose from the dead. He's the only prophet who is still alive."

Dumbfounded, the owner admitted, "I've never heard anything like this. Here is my business card." At the end of our discussion, he accepted copies of some material to help him understand that the Injeel is not corrupted and why Jesus died on the cross.

Jesus calls us to be people of compassion, to show our Muslim friends respect and love. Regardless of his decision, regardless of his attitude, regardless of his response, my job is to be like Jesus and have a spirit of compassion.

The struggle we had at the beginning of our talk is that he wasn't yet ready to hear something different than what he had been taught. He tried to defend himself by being insulting to me. But Jesus calls us to be people of compassion, to show our Muslim friends respect and love. Regardless of his decision, regardless of his attitude, regardless of his response, my job is to be like Jesus and have a spirit of compassion.

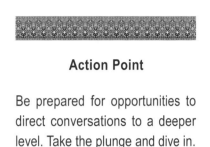

Action Point

Be prepared for opportunities to direct conversations to a deeper level. Take the plunge and dive in.

Islamic Logic About Jesus' Forgiveness

It's important for us to have a solid understanding of what Muslims believe about how sin is forgiven. Many Muslims think that Christians are lazy and morally loose, leading them to sin. That Jesus forgives sinners of their sin without requiring any act to compensate for the sin is seen as insensible. Muslims think that Jesus' being punished for others' sins is completely illogical. They pride themselves in their righteous acts that will erase their sins on Judgment Day.

For Muslims, life is a test, and on Judgment Day your individual good works will earn you a place in paradise. They see God as a just judge, who is also a great businessman. One cannot steal from him. So punishing Jesus Christ for the sins of man does not fit into their sense of God's justice.

Confusion About the Cross

The characteristic Muslim perspective about Jesus' death on the cross is that Jesus didn't actually die on the cross. Instead, he was lifted to heaven to escape his enemies, and someone else was crucified instead. Therefore, Christians are mistaken in believing that Jesus died on the cross. In accordance with Muslim belief, God sends prophets to enlighten people, and so death is not a means of enlightening others. Muslims maintain that Christians have incorrect information about the life of Christ.

Muhammad, however, defeated the enemies of Islam and destroyed the idols in the Ka'aba, making him triumphant over Jesus. For Muslims, God's prophet must win and be victorious because all of the prophets mentioned in the Qur'an won and overcame their adversaries. Therefore, Jesus must also "win" as a prophet of God. According to Muslims, Jesus as the messenger of God cannot lose, and dying on a cross is not a victory, but a defeat.

Action Point

Know what Muslims believe about Christians and Christ. You can start even by asking a Muslim friend what he or she believes personally.

Throughout the known world, the early Christians proclaimed the good news of Jesus Christ. They declared the crucified Jesus as the Messiah, which was foolishness to the Gentiles and a stumbling block for the Jews (1 Corinthians 1:23). The Gentiles were asking for wisdom, and the Jews were asking for a sign. But where is the wisdom of the cross? Why would the Messiah die for our sins?

For Muslims, Jesus was sent by God and must not lose by dying, but win. Islam criticizes the crucifixion, proclaiming instead that Jesus did not die on the cross, but rather that someone else died there. In Islamic history, there have been five main theories about who died on the cross.

- Judas instead of Jesus: The most common idea about who actually died on the cross is that Judas Iscariot was taken by God and changed to look like Jesus. Therefore, because he looked like Jesus, the Roman soldiers crucified the wrong person.

- The Jewish bystander: The second theory is that God took a Jewish bystander, someone walking on the street, and changed him to look like Jesus. This man died on the cross. The Romans crucified the wrong Jewish man.

- A Roman soldier: A third theory asserts that a Roman soldier was changed to look like Jesus and died on the cross.

- The disciple Peter: A fourth theory says that one of the disciples, probably Peter, volunteered to be crucified instead. He was then changed to look like Jesus and was crucified in Christ's place.

- Jesus hung on the cross but never died (the "swoon theory"): The swoon theory claims that Jesus did not die on the cross, but instead "swooned" or fainted. In the tomb, Jesus was revived, and he pushed the two-ton stone aside, scared the soldiers guarding the tomb, and moved to the Indian subcontinent where he raised a family. The Ahmadiyyah sect of Islam generally argues in favor of this theory. They use it to validate their founder, Ghulam Ahmad.

GOING BACK TO THE SOURCE

These contradicting theories show us that there's no clear understanding about what happened to Jesus, the son of Mary, *unless* we turn to the Injeel. The Injeel is clear about what happened to the Messiah Jesus: Jesus died on the cross and he rose from the dead to redeem all people, all in fulfillment of the prophecy.

When I was growing up, I had to make a decision. I decided Islam was not the religion for me because Islam says, "During your life, do this, this and that, and perhaps you will get to heaven." For me, this was not good enough. First, I refuse to ride a plane that says "maybe" you will get to your destination. Second, I'm not going to ride a plane that doesn't have an engine, even if the outside of the plane looks sleek and shiny. The plane I'm going to ride must have an engine, and for me, that engine is made up of facts.

If the Bible is the Word of God, it has to be backed up by facts that it was not corrupted. Because if Jesus was not born of the Virgin Mary, and the whole story of who he is is false, then what am I standing on? If Jesus did not die on the cross and rise from the dead, then on what grounds can I defend my faith? We need to answer who died on the cross from the facts in the Bible. The Bible is our foundation, our source—not the imams or religious leaders.

So what glorifies God more? To help Jesus escape death, or to help Jesus conquer death? Clearly, when he conquers death, he glorifies God. Jesus in the Injeel is mentioned as the *Al-Ghaleb*— the Conqueror, the Victorious One—because he conquered Satan, sin and death. Jesus performed a spiritual conquering. He rose from the dead to show that God accepted his sacrifice. Christ was also the Redeemer, *Al-Fadi*, the Savior, because his redemption was for all people to save them from sin. He was the Lamb of God who takes away the sins of the world.

To respond to our Muslim friends in a loving, biblical way, we must be prepared to answer their questions about Jesus and the cross. A key place to begin is to explain that Christians believe that God is holy and that all humans are sinful. For it is written, "There is no one righteous, not even one" (Romans 3:10). Indeed, we are a people in need of a Savior.

Continually returning to the Injeel for truths about Jesus' death and resurrection will give us valuable insights to help in our conversations with our Muslim friends.

The righteousness of Christ. We can agree with our Muslim friends that God is a just judge and that a sinner cannot redeem another sinner. Jesus Christ was righteous, sinless from birth. He conquered both sin and Satan and therefore can intercede to redeem all humanity. Through the shedding of his blood, he paid the debt we owe to God: "This is my blood of the covenant, which is poured out for many for the forgiveness of sins" (Matthew 26:28). He is the true Adha sacrifice. *Adha* is an Arabic word meaning "sacrifice." Muslims celebrate *Eid Al-Adha* to remember the redemption of Abraham's son with a sheep. The sheep died, and the son of Abraham was saved. Likewise, Jesus is our Redeemer, our Adha, our Passover!

The power of the resurrection. Christ rose from the dead, having conquered both sin and Satan. His resurrection proves the power of God and that Jesus is victorious over the enemies of God. It is proof that Christ was righteous and his sacrifice was acceptable to God. Through the Holy Spirit he "was appointed the Son of God in power by his resurrection from the dead: Jesus Christ our Lord" (Romans 1:4).

Keep in mind that our Muslim friends believe that Christ's death rendered defeat. But the Injeel always mentions crucifixion *and* the resurrection at the same time: it is a chronicle of *seeming* defeat turned into the ultimate victory. Jesus did not lose by dying; he won through his resurrection from the dead.

In all of history, no human has ever risen from the dead to live forever. Jesus is the only Prophet who is still alive today. Because he is alive we can share in the salvation he offers. In his letter to the Philippians, Paul writes, "I want to know Christ—yes, to know the power of his resurrection and participation in his sufferings, becoming like him in his death, and so, somehow,

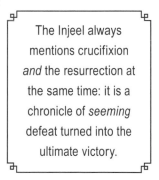

The Injeel always mentions crucifixion *and* the resurrection at the same time: it is a chronicle of *seeming* defeat turned into the ultimate victory.

attaining to the resurrection from the dead" (Philippians 3:10-11).

New life, eternal salvation. God offers us an incredible opportunity to share in a new life through belief in Jesus Christ. "Praise be to the God and Father of our Lord Jesus Christ! In his great mercy he has given us new birth into a living hope through the resurrection of Jesus Christ from the dead" (1 Peter 1:3). Eternal forgiveness can be experienced if we come to God through the redemption of Christ. The book of Romans tells us how we can be sure of our salvation: "If you declare with your mouth, 'Jesus is Lord,' and believe in your heart that God raised him from the dead, you will be saved. For it is with your heart that you believe and are justified, and it is with your mouth that you profess your faith and are saved" (Romans 10:9-10).

Action Point

Have a personal plan about how you can explain to your Muslim friend how he or she can have assurance of salvation. Consider memorizing a few key verses to help you.

Sure of our salvation. This is a completely distinctive idea from salvation in Islam, where being sure of your salvation is impossible. Our Muslim friends are hoping beyond hope that their good works will ensure their salvation. But we know that salvation comes from the Lord himself. "For it is by grace you have been saved, through faith—and this is not from yourselves, it is the gift of God—not by works, so that no one can boast" (Ephesians 2:8-9).

The only way. We must share this news with Muslims. Respectfully, we can ask them what would happen to their salvation if on Judgment Day the scale is 50/50. The Injeel is clear that Jesus is the only way to salvation: "Salvation is found in no one else, for there is no other name under heaven given to mankind by which we must be saved" (Acts 4:12).

Sometimes our friends will think we are eccentric for believing that Jesus is the only way. I have a family friend who is diabetic. She has to use insulin to keep her body healthy. It would sound crazy if I went to her doctor and said, "You know, Doctor, you are pretty eccentric. Lighten up. Why give her insulin all the time? Just give her apple pie one day." What do you think the doctor would tell me? He would tell me, "Listen, buddy, the only cure, the only solution for your friend's health situation, is insulin. She absolutely requires it."

> As believers in Christ, we have the cure for sin. The only cure is Jesus. The struggle today is that people are determined to find their own way.

As believers in Christ, we know the cure for a disease much worse than diabetes. We have the cure for sin. The only cure is Jesus. The struggle today is that people are determined to find their own way.

THE WISDOM OF THE CROSS

The resurrection could have been easily disproved. All the Jewish or Roman leaders had to do was bring the body of Jesus forward, but *no one* had the body of Jesus because the tomb was empty— Christ rose from the dead. Like the early disciples of Christ, we must tell everyone that Jesus was born of the Virgin Mary, that he lived a perfect life, gave us great teaching, died on the cross for our redemption and rose from the dead for our justification.

The sign of salvation was the resurrection so that all can come to faith in Jesus Christ. But the wisdom of the cross is the redemption of mankind. *Al-Masih qam; haqan qam!* (He is risen! He has risen, indeed!)

> Closing prayer: *Our heavenly Father, thank you that you are glorified in the resurrection. Hallelujah! You provided the greatest miracle. I thank you for my Redeemer. In Christ's name, amen.*

Chapter 9

Don't Christians Worship
Three Gods?

In the beginning was the Word, and the Word
was with God, and the Word was God.

JOHN 1:1

—●—

THE TRINITY: A MATH PROBLEM?

Three Muslim men attended our youth group meeting one
evening. From their appearance, they were conservative, and
they said they were studying to become Muslim sheikhs (religious leaders). They told us they were learning to debate Christians, so they wanted to sit down and debate us that evening. We
welcomed them into the meeting not to debate them, but rather
to share Christ and his teachings.

As we all sat back down at the table, the head of the meeting
politely informed them, "We will answer your questions, but we
won't debate." They said, "Sure. So why do you believe in God,
Jesus and Mary?"

Realizing what the Muslim men were actually saying, the
leader replied, "Well, we don't believe in God, Jesus and Mary as

three gods. We believe in God the Father, God the Son and God the Holy Spirit." Puzzled, the Muslim men countered, "That still doesn't make sense. One plus one plus one equals three."

Have you already been asked by your Muslim friends why Christians believe in three gods? It's a common misinterpretation of the Christian Trinity. Many Muslims think that Christians worship God the Father, Jesus the Son and Mary the mother.

Pre-Islamic Arabian paganism is partly to blame for this misconception. The problem is, the idea has endured and many Muslims understand the Christian Trinity to be a form of tritheism. Therefore, the Trinity is a form of blasphemy (*Al-Kufr*), for in this model others are associated as being equal with God (*Al-Shirk*).

DEFINING THE INJEEL

The Qur'an explicitly states that one cannot claim that God is three. Muslim logic demands that God is one and that absolute unity is one. From a Muslim perspective, the idea of having three forms of God means that one plus one plus one equals three, which is blasphemy. It is up to us to share the truth about the Trinity with our Muslim friends to correct their mistaken beliefs. It is our responsibility to delineate the Injeel.

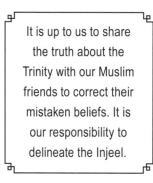

It is up to us to share the truth about the Trinity with our Muslim friends to correct their mistaken beliefs. It is our responsibility to delineate the Injeel.

We don't approach the Pope to define the Qur'an; we go to Muslims to define the Qur'an. Likewise, we must not let Muslims define the Injeel; we must define the Injeel. A significant problem today with reaching Muslims is that we not only allow them to define Islam, but we also allow them the freedom to define Christianity. The biblical foundation is what Christians use to define their beliefs.

Contrary to popular belief, Muslims respect us more when we stand up for what we believe and when we set boundaries about how we will discuss our faith.

Action Point

Defend your faith by defining the teachings of the Injeel for your Muslim friends. You will earn their respect.

BRIDGING TO THE TRINITY IN THE INJEEL

There are many approaches to sharing truth about the Trinity with your Muslim friends. One such way is to listen to what they have to say about the Trinity, and then respond with respect, "Well, that's a good point but let me share with you what the Bible says." We always want to remain loving, friendly, bridging and biblical. So point your friend to what the Injeel has to say about the Trinity.

The word *Trinity* is a human term to explain the character of God revealed in the Injeel. While human logic will never understand the complexity of God's character, it is imperative that we engage with who God says he is in the Bible.

THE ONENESS OF GOD

We believe that God is one and cannot be divided, nor mutilated, nor multiplied. While Islam teaches a simple oneness of God (*Al-Tawhid*), Christianity celebrates a complex oneness of God: God the Father, God the Son and God the Holy Spirit. There is no difference between any of the three persons of God. We believe in this doctrine, though it is above our reason, because the Injeel clearly states it. Jesus

> While human logic will never understand the complexity of God's character, it is imperative that we engage with who God says he is in the Bible.

himself declared, "Therefore go and make disciples of all nations, baptizing them in the name of the Father and of the Son and of the Holy Spirit" (Matthew 28:19).

Al-Tawhid (oneness) in the Injeel is based on the oneness of God who exists with his Word and his Spirit through all eternity. You might ask, Who existed first: God, his Word or his Spirit? Some may say that it was God who existed first, but that doesn't make sense because that means that he existed without his Word or his Spirit. From the beginning to the end of time, God exists with his Word. God's Word became Jesus, and his Spirit is the Holy Spirit. Muslims tend to argue that 1 + 1 + 1 = 3, but I say instead that 1 x 1 x 1 = 1. No human measurement can ever capture God's nature and God's character. God revealed himself through the Bible and ultimately through Jesus Christ. We are not expected to completely comprehend the nature of God. But we are expected to experience his revelation and enjoy him forever.

> **Action Point**
>
> Acknowledge your Muslim friend's point of view, and then point them back to the Bible. Read Bible verses with them so as to impart biblical concepts and understanding.

DIFFERENCES IN THE TRINITY

What's the difference between God, his Word and his Spirit? Jesus is the bodily incarnation of God. On the cross, it wasn't God dying, it was God incarnate. It was Jesus, the Son of God, dying; death is when the spirit leaves the body. The body of Christ was broken for us; the spirit still lived. And that's where many times we mess up in our communication with Muslims, because the best wording is that Jesus is the Incarnate God, God's Word become flesh. On the cross, God's Son, the Redeemer and Messiah, carried our debts.

Jesus said, "[The Spirit of truth] will glorify me because it is from me that he will receive what he will make known to you" (John 16:14). The Spirit of God is the Holy Spirit. He is equal with God and equal with the Word. The Spirit of God leads us and glorifies Jesus. The Word of God became Jesus, who limited himself, which is addressed in the books of Ephesians and Philippians. He humbled himself; he came to us. God reached out to humans! This act of incarnation helps all Christians to articulate the gospel better. Our position is, "No human can experience the awesomeness of God; we cannot touch God. He has to come to us. He has to limit himself in Christ to clearly reveal his will."

This makes sense to us as Christians, and if you explain it clearly to your Muslim friends, it will make sense to them as well. It's going to take time, but if you are loving and friendly, and you are bridging and biblical, they will understand. They will come to Christ, recognizing that Christ is the Savior. There's no one else who can save them. Be patient. Explain the greatness of God who exists from eternity to eternity with his Word and Spirit. We cannot comprehend the greatness of the Creator through our finite mind.

MODELS TO ILLUSTRATE

Though any earthly model cannot fully capture the nature of God or the nature of the Trinity, you might find it helpful to explain how Christians view God. You might choose examples that are natural or logical, like thinking of God in terms of multiplication instead of addition; the makeup of the sun, including the sun's light, warmth and rays; or an equilateral triangle, in which all three sides of the triangle are equal but necessarily distinct.

You could also explain that water is needed for life. H_2O is the chemical symbol for water. Three atoms make up one molecule: two hydrogen atoms and one oxygen atom form one molecule of water. Wherever you find water, whether in the form of liquid, solid or vapor, you find H_2O. Taking one atom or adding an atom changes the whole substance. We humans cannot completely comprehend that. How does a whole substance change just by changing one atom? If we cannot fully grasp this, how much more are we unable to grasp God's character and nature?

God's nature is divine. It's above all reason. We humans cannot completely understand the nature of our Creator. But these analogies can be helpful tools for us and our Muslim friends to move toward understanding.

A Kindly Challenge

Remember those Muslim men who wanted to debate with Christians at the youth group meeting? Our dialogue continued once they concluded their statement that using addition was not an acceptable explanation for how Christians worship three gods.

I responded to them, "That's a good point, but you are trying to understand God's character, and none of us will be able to do that. We're humans; we're limited. God's character is above our reason. For example, if you are explaining fusion and fission of the nuclear bomb to someone who's in fifth grade, he won't understand much. The problem is not that what you're saying goes against logic. The problem is that what you're trying to explain is above his logic. The same student will under-

Action Point

Have a bank of illustrations handy, either in your mind or on paper, to help your Muslim friends understand the Trinity. *Trinity* is a human word to explain the nature of God as revealed to us in the Bible.

stand fusion and fission later as his logic grows with education."

After considering my points for a minute, one of the men answered, "How can you still say God the Son, God the Father, and God the Holy Spirit is one?" I leaned in.

"Instead of only applying addition to God, why don't we apply multiplication? Think about it this way: one times one times one equals one."

Within seconds, his eyes lit up. Suddenly he spoke aloud, "Oh!" What hit him was that he was trying to understand God in earthly, human ideas, and God is neither earthly nor human.

As he was a man learning to debate with Christians, our new Muslim friend was not going to capitulate without a struggle. He quickly rejoined, "But the Bible is corrupted." Was I happy when he said that? Of course! It was important for me to show him that his disagreement with the Trinity was not that it's illogical, but that the Bible has been changed. His admission that he thinks the Bible's been corrupted just revealed that his concerns about the Trinity were merely a smoke screen.

> The logic of the Trinity is far above our logic. It is God's domain. How he is one, we don't understand. But we believe it because the Bible teaches it, and we must seek to understand it and explain it as clearly as we're able.

Since the men were at the meeting to argue, none of them asked for a copy of the Injeel, but by the end of the discussion, I reached a point of understanding with the most outspoken of the men: he didn't believe the Bible is the Word of God. That was the real issue. If he did, then the Trinity would be relatively easy to believe in.

The logic of the Trinity is far above our logic. It is God's domain. How he is one, we don't understand. But we believe it because the Bible teaches it, and we must seek to understand it and explain it as clearly as we're able.

THE BRIDGING APPROACH

By directing our Muslim friends to the Injeel, we act in a biblical, friendly way. Using this approach, we build bridges. We bridge minds by sharing the illustrations we have that help us understand such a difficult concept as the Trinity.

However, we must exercise caution and discretion. There is a distinct difference between illustrating and understanding. If we claim to understand God, we indicate that we are above God. But God is far above us. Our job is to show our friends that their lines of thinking are not working. In the end, they have to come back to what the Word of God says. We can point them there. We must point them there.

> There is a distinct difference between illustrating and understanding. If we claim to understand God, we indicate that we are above God. And God is far above us.

Closing prayer: *Our heavenly Father, thank you for creating me. Thank you for your Word Jesus who redeemed me! Thank you for your Holy Spirit who sustains me. In Christ's name, amen.*

Chapter 10

Why Did Jesus Have to Be Sacrificed?

Al-Adha *in the Injeel*

For God so loved the world that he gave his one and only Son,
that whoever believes in him shall not perish
but have eternal life.

JOHN 3:16

—●—

IF A PERSON'S GOOD WORKS are "good enough" to get into heaven, as most Muslims believe, then what need is there for a sacrifice for sins? Because Muslims pride themselves in their righteous acts, which they expect will erase their sins on Judgment Day, they find Christianity to be illogical in punishing Jesus for the sins of others. Even more, punishing Jesus Christ for our sins does not fit with God's justice. God is a just judge. He is accurate in all his records of human deeds—therefore, according to Muslims, there is no need for a sacrifice to atone for sins because God already knows what sins were committed.

GOOD WORKS AND GOD'S JUSTICE

If a friend of mine asks me to watch his house while he travels, he expects me to take good care of his possessions. But let's say that while he is gone, I accidentally destroy the furniture. To make up for my lapse in judgment, I wash his car as a gesture of goodwill. Does washing his car cover the cost of replacing the furniture? No! If I ask my friend to have mercy and forgive me for destroying his furniture since I washed the car, is it acceptable? Of course not!

> Our good works are not righteous enough compared to God's righteousness. Our good works will never erase sin, for we are expected to do good and obey God's commandments.

Even if he forgave me, my friend still has to pay for new furniture. Likewise, our good works are not righteous enough compared to God's righteousness. Our good works will never erase sin, for we are expected to do good and obey God's commandments.

In contrast to a Muslim's perspective, a Christian standpoint sees God as holy and all humans as sinful. No one is righteous in the sight of God. Sin must be punished by death, an eternal separation from God. All are in need of salvation through an eternal sacrifice. Only Jesus Christ was sinless from birth and conquered sin and Satan. As the Word of God, Jesus is the only one who can intercede for and redeem all humanity.

Action Point

Be aware of other Muslim holidays and celebrations through which you can create a bridge to the gospel. For example, the yearly Hajj could be an opportunity to discuss how sins are forgiven through a Christian perspective.

MUSLIMS AND *AL-ADHA*

The concept of sacrifice is not new to Muslims. In fact, every year Muslims around the world celebrate the feast of *Al-Adha*, which takes place seventy days after the end of Ramadan, on the tenth of *Dhul-Hijat*, a month of the Muslim lunar calendar. The root word for *Adha* is the Arabic word *Dahiya*, which means "sacrifice." The *Al-Adha* feast is also known as the Feast of Sacrifice, or the Great Feast, the *Eid Al-Kabir*.

At the *Al-Adha* feast, many Muslims sacrifice a sheep to commemorate the holy event when God redeemed the son of Abraham. When Abraham was about to sacrifice his son, the angel of the Lord stopped him. Abraham looked and saw a ram caught in the thicket by its horns. He took the ram and sacrificed it as a burnt offering. The full record of this event is found in the *Tawrat*, in Genesis 22:1-19. In Islam, this occurrence is recorded in the Qur'an in Surat Al-Saffat (37): 99-111. When Muslims celebrate the *Eid Al-Adha*, they recognize in their commemoration that a blessing happened and that there was a celebration because a sheep died in the place of Abraham's son. There was a *redemption*.

Although the Jewish religion does not commemorate this specific event with a feast, the same idea and meaning are included in the Passover that was given to them by the prophet Moses. Jews celebrate the Passover to commemorate the night that God spared the Jewish firstborn from being slain in Egypt. The angel of death passed over the houses of those who put the blood of a slaughtered sheep at their doorposts, without harming their firstborn. The Passover is recorded in the *Tawrat*, in Exodus 12:1-14.

IS THERE A CHRISTIAN ADHA?

Since Christians believe in both the Passover and the Adha events, why don't they celebrate them? Is there a Christian Passover too? To answer these questions, we need to look to the

Injeel and examine its teachings on the character of God and his plan for mankind.

God is love. God is the creator of the universe and seeks fellowship with his creation. God's joy and pleasure is to communicate with humans, the highest of creation, bestowed with both a mind and a will. God created us to commune with him and to have fellowship with him. "God is love. Whoever lives in love lives in God, and God in them" (1 John 4:16). Jesus says that he came so that we would enjoy the fullness of life: "I have come that they may have life, and have it to the full" (John 10:10). Since God seeks fellowship with humans, why is our world so far from God? Why do people feel separated from God? It seems as if a great gulf separates us from enjoying God and his love.

God's holiness versus sin. All humans fall short of perfectly obeying God's standard and law. Since the days of Adam, all people have chosen to go their own way rather than to obey God. This disobedience is what the Injeel calls sin.

God is holy and righteous, and humans are sinful. Everywhere we turn, we see the sinfulness of humans. Our actions are symptoms of the real disease of sin. We can also describe sin as rebellion against God—essentially choosing our way instead of God's way.

We have all sinned against God Almighty and we cannot remove our guilt. The Injeel affirms that all have sinned against a holy God:

> There is no one righteous, not even one;
>> there is no one who understands;
>> there is no one who seeks God.
> All have turned away,
>> they have together become worthless;
> there is no one who does good,
>> not even one. (Romans 3:10-12)

God is just. The Injeel continues to explain that sin is what separates us from our loving and holy God, because a righteous God is holy and cannot fellowship with sinful people. God's holiness condemns sin. Therefore, God and

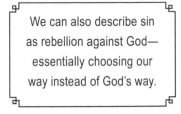

We can also describe sin as rebellion against God— essentially choosing our way instead of God's way.

humans have been separated by a great gulf, which is sin, a separation from God that results in spiritual death. The very righteous character of God cannot accept sin, "for the wages of sin is death" (Romans 6:23). Sin has made us spiritually dead, lifeless and aimless.

God's justice compels him to punish and destroy sin. God cannot forgive a sinful person until that sinful person's debt is paid. Mere good works such as fasting or giving alms to the poor cannot pay the debt by earning God's favor. The noblest of acts fall short of God's perfect holiness and justice. Our very best is not good enough to please a perfect God, which means every single person—even the best of us—has sinned and must be punished.

God is merciful. So how can we return to God if we know that everyone has sinned and falls short of the glory of God? God's mercy sought to provide an answer to this problem. God wants to fellowship with us, his creation. Only a righteous person can cross over the gulf to God.

Enter Jesus Christ, the only sinless man on earth. The Injeel teaches that Jesus is the only bridge between a holy God and sinful humans.

Miraculous life. Jesus Christ lived a life of purity and honesty. He was obedient to the laws of God throughout his life. Jesus taught like no one else and miraculously healed every weakness and disease. He was sinless from birth and was considered the greatest teacher that ever lived.

Jesus went throughout Galilee, teaching in their synagogues, proclaiming the good news of the kingdom, and healing every disease and sickness among the people. News about him spread all over Syria, and people brought to him all who were ill with various diseases, those suffering severe pain, the demon-possessed, those having seizures, and the paralyzed; and he healed them. Large crowds from Galilee, the Decapolis, Jerusalem, Judea and the region across the Jordan followed him. (Matthew 4:23-25)

Miraculous death: **Al-Adha** *in the Injeel.* Jesus did not come to earth merely to be a good teacher or healer. He came specifically to be the sacrifice of God. Because Jesus is righteous, sinless from birth, his death alone can pay the penalty for sin. He came to redeem humanity from its fallen state. The Injeel clearly states that all have sinned against God and are in need of salvation. Salvation means to be pardoned by God because someone paid the penalty that we could not pay ourselves.

As we have emphasized, humans are dead in sin. Sin is the gulf that separates us from God. Jesus Christ was crucified, and died as a righteous sacrifice for the human race. Just as Abraham sacrificed a ram instead of his son, Jesus willingly gave up his life on the cross as a sacrifice to pay the penalty of the sin of all mankind. The sheep died so the son of Abraham may be set free. Likewise, Jesus died so we can be set free. For as God redeemed the son of Abraham with a ram, likewise God redeemed the world through Jesus Christ.

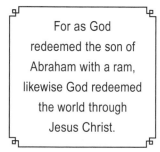

For as God redeemed the son of Abraham with a ram, likewise God redeemed the world through Jesus Christ.

As Muslims sacrifice a sheep during the *Eid Al-Adha,* and the Israelites sacrificed a sheep during Passover in Egypt, so God made Jesus Christ the perfect sacrifice for our sins. Jesus became the true Adha. He was the Lamb of God to lift away the sins of the world. John the Baptist, known as the prophet "Yahya" in the Qur'an, prophesied when he saw Jesus: "Look, the Lamb of God, who takes away the sin of the world!" (John 1:29).

Through Jesus Christ, God bridged the gulf that separated us from him. Paul said in his letter to the Corinthians, "All this is from God, who reconciled us to himself through Christ and gave us the ministry of reconciliation" (2 Corinthians 5:18). The justice of God was satisfied, for the penalty of sin was paid. The mercy of God was satisfied, for humans have redemption.

Miraculous resurrection. Because Jesus is righteous, he did not deserve death. He is the Word of God, the *Kalimat Allah*, who became the sacrifice for our salvation. Christ's resurrection from the dead on the third day, all according to the prophecy, proved that his sacrifice was acceptable to God. The Injeel testifies to the resurrection of Christ:

Action Point

If you ever have the opportunity to attend a Muslim feast, do so. Prepare yourself in advance about how to dress and how to behave, but bask in the unique chance to witness firsthand how your Muslim friends understand and live out their beliefs. It will be a rich learning experience you'll never forget. Pray that God will use this time to shine your light to others.

> For what I received I passed on to you as of first importance: that Christ died for our sins according to the Scriptures, that he was buried, that he was raised on the third day according to the Scriptures, and that he appeared to Cephas, and then to the Twelve. After that, he appeared to more than five hundred of the brothers and sisters at the

same time, most of whom are still living, though some have fallen asleep. (1 Corinthians 15:3-6)

At Easter, Christians around the world celebrate the Adha and the Passover in one glorious celebration of the crucifixion and resurrection of Jesus Christ. This is the Adha and Passover come true!

BRIDGING THE ADHA

Only the Christian Adha covers the debt of our sin and bridges the gap between us and God. The important issue to discuss with Muslims is the substitutionary role of Christ—what we call the redemption, or the sacrifice. Jesus is the true Adha sacrifice. He paid the debt humanity owed to God.

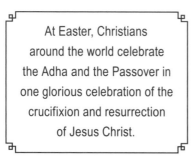

At Easter, Christians around the world celebrate the Adha and the Passover in one glorious celebration of the crucifixion and resurrection of Jesus Christ.

Because of Christ's sacrifice, we are able to experience eternal forgiveness from God. Use this bridge to show why John the Baptist called Jesus the Lamb of God who took on the sins of the world. Christ became our Lamb; he became our Redeemer. He took our sin. So when we approach God, we come through Christ's name, through his sacrifice, through his work.

This is why Easter is such an important celebration for us, because we commemorate how we are released from our sins, and that through Christ's sacrifice the door to God is open to us. God is holy and mighty, and he can help us because we are living according to his commands through faith in Christ as our Savior.

GOD IS FORGIVING

It is not enough to know that God has provided the Adha for sin. Each one of us needs to receive this sacrifice in a personal and humble decision. We must repent and receive Jesus Christ as Lord and Savior in order to experience God's love and forgiveness.

Repentance is turning to God from our own sinful ways and receiving God's offer of forgiveness made possible by Christ's work on the cross, what we call here the Christian Adha. The Injeel promises us, "If we confess our sins, he is faithful and just and will forgive our sins and purify us from all unrighteousness" (1 John 1:9). God forgives our sins if we confess them, because Christ paid the debt.

The Christian Adha released us from spiritual death and offered us eternal life. God's gift of eternal life is in accepting Christ's sacrifice. We receive Christ's sacrifice by faith. It is free, but it is priceless. We can do nothing to earn it ourselves. Like any gift, the ultimate gift of God cannot be enjoyed unless it is *received.* We receive Christ and his sacrificial work by a personal commitment. Use opportunities of open doors with your Muslim friends to invite them to personally receive the gift of God, which is eternal salvation through Christ.

Christ is seeking to enter our lives, cleanse us from sin and mend our broken relationship with God. Christ wants to be our Lord and Savior. Jesus invites us to open the doors of our heart to him: "Here I am! I stand at the door and knock. If anyone hears my voice and opens the door, I will come in" (Revelation 3:20).

PRAYER TO RECEIVE JESUS

Remember that prayer for Muslims is often little more than a recitation of phrases. But for Christians, prayer is a means of talking directly to God. It's a way to have open communication with him. We can pray to God wherever we are and whenever we want. To receive Christ's sacrifice, we are to pray to God and in faith know that we have salvation.

Offer your Muslim friends opportunities to receive Jesus

Christ through prayer. You can lead them through a simple prayer like this one: "Dear Lord, thank you for your love to me. I ask your forgiveness because of Christ's atoning death. I open the door of my life and receive Jesus Christ as my Lord and Savior. Make me a new person. Thank you for giving me eternal life. In Jesus' name. Amen."

By asking Christ to enter their life, our Muslim friends, too, can have their sins forgiven and can be restored to fellowship with God.

JESUS' FAITHFULNESS

The Injeel teaches that Jesus Christ is faithful to his promises. He tells us, "If you remain in me and my words remain in you, ask whatever you wish, and it will be done for you" (John 15:7). We not only can trust him to answer prayer, but we also can trust that he will never abandon us: "Never will I leave you; never will I forsake you" (Hebrews 13:5). The Lord promises to be with us in every step of our journey. "Being confident of this, that he who began a good work in you will carry it on to completion until the day of Christ Jesus" (Philippians 1:6). Our God is eternal, unwavering in who he is. The writer of Hebrews assures us, "Jesus Christ is the same yesterday and today and forever" (Hebrews 13:8).

Action Point

Don't be afraid to extend an invitation more than once to your Muslim friends to pray to receive Christ.

THE TRUE ADHA

Salvation can only be found through Jesus' sacrifice on the cross, where he broke the barrier of sin that separated us from God and heaven. For Muslims—and the entire world—Jesus is the true Adha.

The Christian Adha is available to everyone, for Christ came to save all people, of all nations and races. Through Christ we can cross over to fellowship with God and experience his eternal love and redemption. We mustn't withhold this good news from our Muslim friends who so desperately need salvation. It is time to overcome any of our fears and boldly share about the Adha who willingly gave up his life for them.

Closing prayer: *Our heavenly Father, thank you for putting such a great example of redemption in the Islamic faith. Thank you for using me to bridge the gospel to their hearts. In Christ's name, amen.*

Chapter 11

Is the Gospel of Barnabas True?

*The woman said, "I know that the Messiah" (called Christ) "is
coming. When he comes, he will explain everything to us."*

Then Jesus declared, "I, the one speaking to you—I am he."

JOHN 4:25-26

⸺●⸺

ONE OF THE EASIEST BRIDGING POINTS we have to make with
our Muslim friends is that the Qur'an claims that God sent the
Injeel (Qur'an 2:136; 3:3-5). Even better, Islam's prophet Muhammad instructed his followers to *believe* (read and follow) the
Injeel! For us, as believers in Christ, this is wonderful news. We
have a direct means of inviting our friends
to read the words of Jesus.

However, the connection also draws
an unexpected logic problem for our
Muslim friends. Our friends argue that
since the Qur'an claims that God sent
the Injeel, likewise, the Injeel must
foretell the coming of the Qur'an.

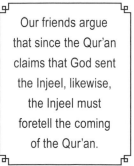

Our friends argue
that since the Qur'an
claims that God sent
the Injeel, likewise,
the Injeel must
foretell the coming
of the Qur'an.

THE GOSPEL OF BARNABAS

When some Muslims read the Injeel, they reason that if the New Testament was given to Jesus, then it must mention Muhammad, because the Qur'an said that Jesus mentioned Muhammad. Then, when Muslims look at the Injeel, they look for a verse in which Jesus said Muhammad is coming after him. But they quickly realize that such a verse doesn't exist.

So what do they do? They begin searching for where such a verse does exist. In Sura 61:6, the Qur'an says, "When Jesus, the son of Mary, said, 'O children of Israel, indeed I am the messenger of Allah to you confirming what came before me of the Torah and bringing good tidings of a messenger to come after me, whose name is Ahmad.' But when he came to them with clear evidences, they said, 'This is obvious magic.'"[1]

Muslim imams then use this verse from the Qur'an and link it to the Gospel of Barnabas, a text the imams claim was written by Barnabas, a contemporary of the apostle Paul. Muslims lean on this text to argue that the Injeel has gone through many versions and the real message has been lost. They claim that the Gospel of Barnabas is the only one that was not corrupted from the Bible. Mostly, however, they like that the Gospel of Barnabas echoes what the Qur'an teaches about Jesus.

OPPOSED TO BOTH CHRISTIANS *AND* MUSLIMS

The fact of the matter is, the Gospel of Barnabas is a false gospel against both Christians *and* Muslims. As I've witnessed to Muslims over the years, I've seen a number of them accept the Gospel of Barnabas at face value. One Muslim guy told me, "I read the true Gospel, the Gospel of Barnabas," just like that. To him, there is no question that the Gospel of Barnabas is fact.

When I meet Muslims who are convinced of the Gospel of Barnabas's authenticity, I usually start by explaining that the

Gospel of Barnabas is false against Muslims *and* Christians. In those situations, somebody will pipe up saying, "What? It's against Muslims *and* Christians?" When I hear that phrase, I know I have an "in" to share more about the fallacies of the Gospel of Barnabas.

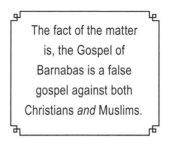

The fact of the matter is, the Gospel of Barnabas is a false gospel against both Christians *and* Muslims.

Discrepancies abound. The core message of the Injeel is that Christ is risen. This is what Christ's disciples went out preaching. Therefore, it stands to reason that if we agree that Christ rose from the dead, then all true Gospels have to follow that same message. And if, as Muslims claim, Barnabas is from the disciples, then he should spread the same message. Also, the author of the Gospel of Barnabas claims to be the Barnabas mentioned in the Bible and an eyewitness to the life of Christ, but this is impossible since the Barnabas of the Bible was from Cyprus.

Not a contemporary. The problem is, the writer of the Gospel of Barnabas was not a disciple of Christ. Most Muslims accept this text assuming the writer was Barnabas the disciple, the friend of Paul. But the writer could not have been that Barnabas because the writer makes mistakes about the geography of the Holy Land. For instance, he claims that Jesus took a boat from Jerusalem to Nazareth (Barnaba 20:1-2; Barnaba is the Arabic title of the work). Anybody who lives in the area knows that it is impossible to take a boat from Jerusalem to Nazareth. So this means that the writer was not only not a contemporary of Jesus Christ, but he was also not even a native of Palestine.

Historical mistakes. The writer also makes mistakes about history. He says that Jesus Christ was born under Pontius Pilate (Barnaba 3:2). Yet it is clear that Jesus was born during the time of Herod the Great. He was *crucified* under Pontius

Pilate. Such an obvious mistake would not be made by a contemporary of Jesus.

Dating problems. If the geographical and historical errors weren't enough, the writer also blunders when it comes to the dating of the manuscript. The manuscript includes quotes from Dante's *Inferno.* How can this be? Dante was born sometime around the 1300s, and so the writer of the Gospel cannot be a contemporary of Jesus. How could he include the same words from the *Inferno* from Dante's comedy, *The Divine Comedy*, a text written in the early fourteenth century? The numbers don't add up.

Moreover, Muslim scholars never mention the Gospel of Barnabas before A.D. 1500. If the Gospel of Barnabas was truly from the days of Jesus, they should have mentioned it. So there is a problem here. If this supposedly true Gospel was such a good, pro-Muslim book, why didn't the Muslim scholars mention it until 1500? It is clear that not only was the text written in the 1300s, but the Muslim scholars weren't even aware of it until 200 years later.

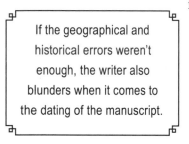

If the geographical and historical errors weren't enough, the writer also blunders when it comes to the dating of the manuscript.

Jubilee jumbles. Even more, in the text the writer says that when Muhammad comes back, the Jubilee year will be celebrated every day, instead of every one hundred years. This throws up a red flag, because the Jubilee year is a Jewish concept. In Jewish tradition, every seven years the land is rested, and after seven "sevens," or the forty-ninth year, the Jubilee year is celebrated. The Jubilee year occurs every fifty years.

So when in history was the Jubilee year celebrated every one hundred years? In the year 1300, Pope Boniface VIII wanted to build the Vatican. So he made a Jubilee year, saying that every one hundred years, all Catholics would donate to the Roman Catholic Church. But when Pope Boniface VIII died, Pope Clement VI succeeded him in 1343. He changed the celebration of the Jubilee year to every fifty years. In 1343, he figured out he'd still be the pope in seven years and that he could finish completing the Vatican by 1350.

Therefore, there is no record of having a Jubilee every one hundred years, besides the time between 1300 and 1343. The writer of the Gospel of Barnabas must have lived during this era, because if he lived after, he would say the Jubilee year was to be celebrated every fifty years. If he lived before this time, he would say the Jubilee year was to be celebrated after forty-nine years. The inconsistencies cannot be overlooked.

Against us both. What tends to floor both Muslims and Christians about the Gospel of Barnabas is that the text posits as facts what we know to be untruths in both Islam and Christianity. That the Gospel of Barnabas is a false testimony against both a biblical view and a Qur'anic view is an important bridge in explaining the truth of the Injeel to our Muslim friends.

Contradictions and childishness. While we know that the writer of the Gospel of Barnabas states fallacies, we perhaps shouldn't deny that he could be rather creative too. The writer states that Muhammad son of Abdallah the prophet of Islam is the Messiah and savior of the world (Barnaba 79:14-18). This is against the Qur'an and

> What tends to floor both Muslims and Christians about the Gospel of Barnabas is that the text posits as facts what we know to be untruths in both Islam and Christianity. That the Gospel of Barnabas is a false testimony against both a biblical view and a Qur'anic view is an important bridge in explaining the truth of the Injeel to our Muslim friends.

the Bible, for they both agree that Jesus of Nazareth was the promised Messiah (Qur'an 4:171; Matthew 16:16).

The writer states that the Messiah will be from the seed of Ishmael, not the seed of David (Barnaba 124:14). Another religious mistake, because for the Messiah to be Jewish, he had to come from the seed of Issac.

The writer states the virgin birth happened without pain (Barnaba 3:5-10), but the Qur'an states that the Virgin Mary did in fact endure labor pains (Qur'an 19:22-23). So how can this be the true Gospel and contradict the Qur'an? What the writer says about the birth of Jesus also goes against the Bible, which states that Mary had a normal childbirth (Luke 2:1-15), and the Qur'an substantiates that she bore labor pains. In one swoop, the Gospel of Barnabas, supposedly a book from God, goes against both the Injeel and the Qur'an.

The writer's errors become more serious as he states that the Old Testament and New Testament were changed (Barnaba 124:8-10). The Qur'an never claims that the Torah and Injeel were changed! This kind of claim from the writer of the Gospel of Barnabas, though, leaves open the possibility that the Qur'an, likewise, might have been changed. These are dangerous waters for the writer to be treading on. The writer is both insulting and defaming the Bible *and* the Qur'an.

Additionally, the writer of the Gospel of Barnabas claims that God is the father of humans (Barnaba 102:18-19), a belief that is unacceptable in both Islam and Christianity. God is not the father of people. God is the *creator* of people, and he is the father of the believers (John 1:12). In Islam, God is the father of no one (Al-Kahf 18:4-3). Again, this false gospel is gravely misconstruing truth from the perspectives of both Christianity and Islam.

In 116:18, the Gospel of Barnabas says that we should marry one wife. That's fine with Christians, but it goes against Muslim beliefs. In Islam, men are permitted to marry up to four wives (Qur'an 4:3). So how can he be supporting the Muslims if he allows only one wife?

The Gospel of Barnabas teaches purgatory, saying that the sinners will go down to hell for only a short time (Barnabas 137:1-4). Purgatory is allowed, and that's against both the Bible and Islam. There is no purgatory according to the Qur'an (Qur'an 33:64-65).

The Gospel writer states that Muhammad is the Messiah, which is wrong. The Bible and the Qur'an both teach that Jesus is the Messiah.

Finally, in the Gospel of Barnabas, there is no mention of John the Baptist. The Injeel says that John the Baptist did exist, and the Qur'an says he existed. The writer of the Gospel of Barnabas uses the language of John the Baptist—"He is the one who comes after me, the straps of whose sandals I am not worthy to untie" (John 1:27)—but omits the person of John the Baptist altogether. He puts the words of John the Baptist in the mouth of Jesus, referring to Muhammad: "Although I am not worthy to unloose the latchet of his shoe" (Barnaba 97:10). Jesus also says in the Gospel of Barnabas, "When I saw Muhammad I was filled with consolation and said : 'O Muhammad, may Allah be with thee and may He make me worthy to unloose the latchet of thy shoe, for if I attain to this I will become a great prophet'" (Barnaba 44:30-31).

In conversations with our Muslim friends, we can show them these problems and read to them 1 John 2:22: "Who is the liar? It is whoever denies that Jesus is the Christ. Such a person is the antichrist—denying the Father and the Son."

THE IDENTITY OF BARNABAS

Muslims who believe that the Gospel of Barnabas is accurate believe it was written by the friend of Paul. Strangely, in this so-called Gospel, Barnabas attacks Paul. How can this be when in the Acts of the Apostles, Barnabas is Paul's best friend? Who took care of Paul? It was Barnabas. Even the fight that is mentioned in the Book of Acts—which was not a fight *between* Paul and Barnabas but concerning John Mark—was not about theology, but about a person and a ministry structure.

So who actually wrote this false gospel under the name of Barnabas? In the foreword to the Gospel of Barnabas, a Roman Catholic priest named Milano claims he found the book. There is an Italian copy and a Spanish copy of the book. The Spanish copy has Andalusian design, indicating that the book was written by a medieval person who lived in Muslim Spain. Probably the priest Milano converted to Islam in Spain under Muslim rulers.

BARNABAS BRIDGES

The Gospel of Barnabas can actually serve as a means of witnessing to your Muslim friends. Full of fallacies and myths, this text is a gold mine for opening up conversations about where Christianity and Islam can *agree*. We can use this false Gospel of Barnabas strategically as a means to create bridges from where the false text goes against both Islam and Christianity.

Presenting how Christ is the true Word of God, plan to share with your Muslim friends that any new "gospel" must agree and build on the Injeel. From there, we can easily bridge to how Jesus of Nazareth is the Messiah, the Christ and long-awaited Redeemer. The doors are opened for us, if we would only walk through them.

> Closing prayer: *Our heavenly Father, thank you that Jesus is your Word become flesh. Thank you for warning us that many false teachers and prophets will come to distract us from following Jesus. Fill me with your Holy Spirit and give me boldness to share your good news. In Jesus' name, amen.*

Chapter 12

Use Your Tools

—●—

WHAT'S IN YOUR TOOLBOX?

Don't we all have tucked away in a garage or closet or even a car trunk a stash of tools that never seem to be used all that much? Maybe for you it's a wrench you needed for one project and then haven't used for a long time. Or perhaps it's a specialty screwdriver that only fits one kind of screw and you don't know how it can be used for other projects.

Sometimes in ministry we have a similar problem. We hone our skills for one kind of ministry and one kind of people, but then we don't really apply those same skills when meeting with new people. Or we only minister to one kind of people for so long that we overlook how we could be opening up compelling conversations with lots of other kinds of people.

Tools are unique instruments, designed with specific purposes in mind. Different tools are designed for different tasks. The same tool must not be used all the time. Its use is appropriate to the task at hand. Likewise, in ministry to Muslims, our use of the same tool again and again results in communication breakdown and frustration. In the hands of skilled laborers, different tools can be used in innovative ways.

What's in your tool stash? What kind of tools do you have tucked away that haven't been used recently? Or how could you use those tools in new ways to reach your Muslim friends and acquaintances?

With Urgency in Mind

In the time it took to read this book, about 6,316 Muslims died without knowing Jesus. And about 15,000 were born into homes in which the family doesn't know Jesus.[1]

I wrote this book, *Connecting with Muslims*, to encourage your faith and to add new approaches to your ministry toolbox. These conversational apologetics are designed to keep the conversation moving to deeper spiritual levels, just like Jesus did.

We absolutely must keep the urgency of the gospel at the forefront of our minds as we reach out to Muslims. It is the purpose of our evangelism. We must look beyond the hijab and beyond the beard to see how thirsty they are for the one true God. We must reap the harvest.

Do Muslims Really Want Jesus?

Our efforts are not in vain. We are seeing the fruits of our labor. In the last fifteen years, more Muslims have come to Christ than in the past *fourteen centuries*. Muslims are seeing the lifestyle of authentic Christians and are finding that lives committed to Jesus are appealing. They have seen the power of God in answered prayers and healing. As they have become dissatisfied with the type of Islam they have experienced over the years, more Muslims are seeing the spiritual truth in the Bible. Biblical teaching about the love of God is reaching Muslims in extraordinary ways.

A Pakistani-American Muslim friend shared what happened to him when he discovered Jesus in the Bible. "My friend would always tell me about Jesus, so when I got my own Bible I would stay up late at night and read it. The Bible taught me so much more than any other religion could. Jesus was different . . . he taught me to turn the other cheek to someone who hit me."

Muslims like my friend are coming to know and follow Jesus all over the world, including North America. Muslims are thirsty for living water!

WATCHING FOR THE NEW THING

Some believers are living under the mistaken belief that Muslims are hard to reach. Too many Christians tend to think Muslims are diametrically opposed to the gospel. They cite immense cultural barriers, anti-Christian beliefs and violent behavior as factors that make Muslims the most difficult group of people to reach with the good news of Jesus.

Historically, that may have been true. But God is doing a new thing among Muslims! God is using the technology explosion, global economy and even wars to bring his people into contact with Muslims.

> See, I am doing a new thing!
> Now it springs up; do you not perceive it? (Isaiah 43:19)

I once watched a debate between a Muslim religious leader and two Christian men on YouTube. I personally don't debate, but God is using this avenue to awaken Muslims to the truth of Christ! Do you think Muslims all over the world aren't tuned into this?

I believe God is calling us to watch for the "new thing" he is doing among Muslims. If we are not looking for it—if we continue to sit on our hands, recalling the former things—will we even perceive it? Will we miss out on his fresh work?

WHAT'S YOUR GOAL?

In our outcome-based culture, we tend to judge the validity of a task by the outcome or goal it accomplishes. But as ambassadors of Jesus, we do not seek to "convert" Muslims. We look to share with them the hope and compassion of Christ. Because Muslims are sometimes taught inaccurate information about Christ and Christians, we want to clear the confusion and share the truth about Christ.

Are we concerned about the outcome? Of course! We rejoice when Muslims hear and understand the gospel and turn to follow Christ. We pray for our friends who reject Christ's message, and we recognize a Muslim's response to the gospel is the result of Christ's work. It cannot be manufactured.

While at a Bible study for internationals, I met Abdallah from Iraq. The study was on Christ's healing the paralyzed man in Matthew 9:1-8. As we discussed the story recorded in the Injeel, I asked, "Could a prophet forgive sins?"

Abdallah answered, "No prophet can forgive sins, only God can!"

I asked, "If Jesus was only a prophet, could he forgive sins?"

Abdallah answered, "Jesus is more than a prophet."

I said, "Abdallah, will you ask God to forgive your sins because of what Jesus did on the cross?"

Abdallah answered that he had been reading the Injeel and that he would like to take Christ as his Savior. Abdallah prayed with the group and decided to follow the Messiah Jesus.

God is moving today. Muslims are open to talk about Christ and his teachings.

So what is *your* goal? What will you now set out to do? We cannot remain at rest while others are perishing. Set realistic, achievable goals for yourself: Meet Muslims. Talk to Muslims. Get into spiritual conversations with Muslims. Welcome Muslims. Be hospitable to Muslims in your home. Visit Muslims. It's time to reap the harvest God puts in your path. Use your tools. *Go.*

Our Messiah Jesus says, "All authority . . . has been given to me. Therefore go and make disciples of all nations" (Matthew 28:18-19).

Closing prayer: *Our heavenly Father, ignite in me a spirit of obedience to Christ. Make me usable in your hand. May I bring glory to your name as I represent you to the Muslims I meet. Here am I, Lord, send me! In Jesus' name, amen.*

Acknowledgments

This book was written as a result of many experiences in building bridges between Christians and Muslims. This book is a resource based on ministry experiences that I have had the privilege of learning about or experiencing myself. I am grateful for the ministry lessons I learned from my father, Adel, and testimonies about my grandfather Issa.

I am thankful for my professors who taught me the Bible and how to communicate the gospel well, especially Dr. Dudley Woodberry and Dr. Kenneth Bailey. I was blessed with the staff team of Crescent Project, who diligently serve our Messiah and supported my efforts to produce this book. I appreciate the guidance that the InterVarsity Press staff offered, especially Al Hsu and his team. Special thanks to Emily Abuatieh for her help in editing and evaluating this document. Finally I am grateful for my family, whose support was invaluable as I wrote this book.

May our Lord Jesus use this resource as a way to equip many Christians to connect with Muslims.

Appendix 1

The Parables of Jesus

TEACHING PARABLES

The Kingdom of God

1. The soils (Matthew 13:3-8; Mark 4:4-8; Luke 8:5-8)

2. The weeds (Matthew 13:24-30)

3. The mustard seed (Matthew 13:31-32; Mark 4:30-32; Luke 13:18-19)

4. The yeast (Matthew 13:33; Luke 13:20-21)

5. The treasure (Matthew 13:44)

6. The pearl (Matthew 13:45-46)

7. The fishing net (Matthew 13:47-50)

8. The growing seed (Mark 4:26-29)

Service and Obedience

1. The workers in the harvest (Matthew 20:1-16)

2. The loaned money (Matthew 25:14-30)

3. The nobleman's servants (Luke 17:7-10)

Prayer

1. The friend at midnight (Luke 11:5-8)

2. The unjust judge (Luke 18:1-8)

Neighbors

1. The good Samaritan (Luke 10:30-37)

Humility

1. The wedding feast (Luke 14:7-11)

2. The proud Pharisee and the corrupt tax collector (Luke 18:9-14)

Wealth

1. The rich fool (Luke 12:16-21)

2. The great feast (Luke 14:16-24)

3. The shrewd manager (Luke 16:1-9)

GOSPEL PARABLES

God's Love

1. The lost sheep (Matthew 18:12-14; Luke 15:3-7)

2. The lost coin (Luke 15:8-10)

3. The lost son (Luke 15:11-32)

Thankfulness

1. The forgiven debts (Luke 7:41-43)

PARABLES OF JUDGMENT AND THE FUTURE

Christ's Return

1. The wise and faithful servants (Matthew 24:45-51; Luke 12:42-48)

2. The ten virgins (Matthew 25:1-13)

3. The traveling owner of the house (Mark 13:34-37)

God's Values

1. The unforgiving servant (Matthew 18:23-35)
2. The two sons (Matthew 21:28-32)
3. The wicked tenants (Matthew 21:33-44; Mark 12:1-9; Luke 20:9-16)
4. The marriage feast (Matthew 22:1-14)
5. The unproductive fig tree (Luke 13:6-9)

Appendix 2

Jesus in the Bible and the Qur'an

Table 1

Title/Description	Qur'an	Bible
Word of God; His [God's] Word (Kalimah)	3:34, 39, 40, 45; 4:169, 171	John 1:1, 14
A Word of truth (Qawl Al-haqq)	19:34, 35	John 4:16; Ephesians 1:13
The Truth from your Lord (Al-haqq)	3:53, 60	John 8:32-36; 14:6
A Spirit of God (Ruh)	4:169, 171; 17; 21:91	Matthew 12:28; Luke 1:35
The Messiah (Al-Masih)	3:40, 45; 4:156, 157	Matthew 16:16; John 1:41
Apostle / Messenger (Rasul)	2:81, 87, 253, 254; 3:43, 49	Hebrews 3:1; Matthew 10:40
Prophet (Nabiyy)	2:130, 136; 4:161, 163	Matthew 21:11; Luke 4:24
Servant of God	4:170, 172; 19:31	Matthew 12:18; John 4:34
Son of Mary (Ibn Maryam)	3:45; 4:157, 171	Luke 2:48
Witness on resurrection day (Shahid)	4:45, 141, 157, 159; 5:117	Matthew 24
Witness of [over] the people	3:120, 117	John 5:36
Mercy from Us [God] (Ramah)	19:21	Matthew 9:27-30
Bearer of wisdom (Hikmah)	43:63	Luke 2:40, 52
Knowledge of the hour ('Ilm)	43:61	Matthew 24:36-44; John 4:25
Sign to all beings (Ayah)	3:44, 50; 19:21; 21:91	Matthew 2:2-11
An example / pattern (Mathal)	43:57, 59	John 13:1-17
The miracle worker	3:49	Mark 1:34; 5:41-42; 6:33-44
Revelation to humankind (Ayah)	19:21	Luke 2:10-12, 30-32
The one to be followed	43:61	John 1:37; 10:27
The one to be obeyed	3:44, 50	Matthew 8:27; 17:5; Mark 1:3
Giver / bringer of good tidings	61:6	Luke 4:18; Acts 10:38
One of the Righteous (min Salihin)	3:40, 46	Matthew 27:19; 2 Timothy 4:1, 8

Knowledgeable in Scriptures	3:43; 48:5, 109, 110	Matthew 12:2-5; John 4:25
Like Adam (*Mathal al Adama*)	3:52, 59	1 Corinthians 15:45-47
The faultless [holy, most pure] Son (*Zakiyy*)	19:19	Luke 23:4, 14, 41; Acts 2:22-36; 1 Peter 2:22-23
One of the closest to God (*Min al Muquarrabi*)	3:40, 41; 7:111, 114	John 14:9-10; Hebrews 2:9

Appendix 3

The Miracles of Jesus

All the recorded miracles of Jesus are listed here in approximate chronological order, with Scripture references. The miracles are grouped according to "healing" miracles and "other" miracles.

Table 2

Healing Miracles				
Recipient	Matthew	Mark	Luke	John
Official's son				4:46-54
Possessed man		1:21-27	4:33-37	
Peter's mother-in-law	8:14-15	1:29-31	4:38-39	
Many at sunset	8:16-17	1:32-39	4:40-41	
Man with leprosy	8:1-4	1:40-45	5:12-15	
Paralytic	9:1-8	2:1-12	5:18-26	
Crippled man at Bethesda				5:1-17
Man with shriveled hand	12:9-13	3:1-6	6:6-11	
Crowd in Galilee	4:23-25			
Centurion's servant	8:5-13		7:1-10	
Widow's son raised			7:11-17	
Possessed man/men	8:28-34	5:1-20	8:26-39	
Jairus's daughter raised	9:18-19, 23-26	5:22-24, 35-43	8:41-42, 49-56	
Woman with bleeding	9:20-22	5:24-34	8:42-48	
Two blind men	9:27-31			
Mute man	9:32-34			
Crowd in Gennesaret	14:34-36	6:53-56		

Crowds in Galilee	9:35			
Few in Nazareth		6:1-6		
Gentile's daughter	15:21-28	7:24-30		
Deaf man		7:31-37		
Multitude	15:29-31			
Epileptic boy	17:14-21	9:14-29	9:37-42	
Blind man				9:1-41
Blind/mute man	12:22-24		11:14-15	
Blind man of Bethsaida		8:22-26		
Crippled woman			13:10-17	
Man with dropsy			14:1-6	
Lazarus raised				11:1-45
Ten lepers			17:11-19	
Crowds in Judea	19:1-2			
Bartimaeus/two blind men	20:29-34	10:46-52	18:35-43	
Many in Jerusalem	21:14			
Ear of Malchus			22:47-53	
Resurrection	28:1-10	16:1-20	24:1-53	20:1-31
Other Miracles				
Event	**Matthew**	**Mark**	**Luke**	**John**
Water to wine				2:1-11
First catch of fish			5:1-11	
Calms a storm	8:23-27	4:35-41	8:22-25	
Feeds five thousand	14:13-21	6:32-44	9:10-17	6:1-13
Walks on water	14:22-33	6:45-51		6:15-21
Feeds four thousand	15:32-39	8:1-10		
Money in fish	17:24-27			
Tree withered	21:18-22	11:12-24		
Second catch of fish				21:1-14

Appendix 4

List of Terms

Abd Allah—a phrase meaning "Servant of God"; also the name of Muhammad's father

Ahmadiyah—an Islamic sect that believes Jesus swooned, rather than died, on the cross

al-tawheed—an Arabic word that means "oneness of God"

amphorae—*amphoreus* in Greek; jars used to hold wine or other liquids

Bible—a book that includes the Tawrat, Zabur and Injeel; it is the holy book of Christianity

Christ—an English word from the Greek word *Christos*, meaning the anointed one or the Messiah; one of the titles of Jesus

Gabriel—one of God's angels, mentioned in both the Qur'an and the Injeel

God—the Almighty Creator of all that is and ever will be

Gospel—a word meaning "truth"

Immanuel—literally, "God with us"; one of the names of Jesus

Injeel—the Arabic name of the Gospel of Jesus, a very important book that Christians call the New Testament

Isa bin Maryam—Arabic for "Jesus son of Mary"; one of the names of Jesus

Isma'il—the Arabic name for Ishmael

Jesus—the Messiah, an important figure in the Qur'an and the Injeel

Jesus Christ—one of the names of Jesus; has the same meaning as "Jesus the Savior" or "Jesus the Messiah"

Joseph—husband of Mary, mother of Jesus; but not Jesus' father

kafir—an Arabic term for unbelieving people who reject the truth

kalimat Allah—the Word of God; one of the names of Jesus

madrasah—religious schools that teach about Islam

Maryam—the Arabic name for Mary, the mother of Jesus

Messiah—a word meaning "savior"; one of the names of Jesus

Mushrik—a person who gives someone equal status with God; an idolater

prophet—a messenger from God

Psalms—another name for the Zabur; songs or hymns

Qur'an—the holy book of Islam

rasul—a title meaning "messenger of God"

Savior—one who saves others; one of the names of Jesus

Son of God—one of the names of Jesus

Son of Mary—one of the names of Jesus

surah—a division of the Qur'an; equivalent to a chapter

Tawrat—the holy books of Moses; also called the Torah

Torah—the holy books of Moses; another name for Tawrat

the Word—one of the names of Jesus

Yahya—John the Baptist, a prophet who told of Jesus' coming

Zabur—the songs of David, also called the Psalms

Appendix 5

Translations of the Bible

The Injeel is the Arabic word used by the Qur'an to refer to the Christians' book known as the New Covenant, or most commonly, the New Testament.

The Injeel was originally written in Koine Greek, the language of the common people in the Roman Empire. Scholars have taken great care to translate the Bible's message into many languages so that people from all nations and backgrounds can understand it.

Some people might accuse translators of changing the meaning of the New Testament. This is very far from the truth. Committees of dedicated scholars ensure that every translation reflects the original Greek texts. Christians consider the Bible a holy book, handling it with respect and honoring the original manuscript in every translation.

In the final analysis, those who doubt the credibility of individual translations should consider studying Koine Greek in order to read the New Testament in its earliest form. In fact, I did that myself. I found the study of the New Testament Greek manuscripts to be fruitful, and intellectually as well as spiritually satisfying. I trust you will find it the same.

Appendix 6

Five Basic Beliefs of All Christians

Did you know that Christians across the world are unified by five core beliefs? We call these the "Five Pillars of Christianity."

1. One God—Christians believe in one God, the creator of the heavens and earth. He is the only one to be worshiped.

"For even if there are so-called gods, whether in heaven or on earth . . . yet for us there is but one God, the Father, from whom all things came and through whom we live." (1 Corinthians 8:5-6)

2. One Savior—Christians believe in one Savior who redeemed all humans. The Messiah Jesus is the Word of God become flesh. He was born of the Virgin Mary and was sinless from birth. His death and resurrection saves us from our sin.

"[Grace] has now been revealed through the appearing of our Savior, Christ Jesus, who has destroyed death and has brought life." (2 Timothy 1:10)

3. One Spirit—Christians are filled and empowered by the Holy Spirit. The Holy Spirit is the Spirit of God that indwells and empowers all Christians to live a godly life.

"But you will receive power when the Holy Spirit comes on you; and you will be my witnesses in Jerusalem, and in all Judea and Samaria, and to the ends of the earth." (Acts 1:8)

4. One Message—Christians are unified by one message. The message of the Injeel (the New Testament) is the basis of all the beliefs of Christians.

"Jesus went into Galilee, proclaiming the good news of God. 'The time has come,' he said. 'The kingdom of God has come near. Repent and believe the good news!'" (Mark 1:14-15)

"All Scripture is God-breathed and is useful for teaching, rebuking, correcting and training in righteousness, so that the servant of God may be thoroughly equipped for every good work." (2 Timothy 3:16-17)

5. One Family—Christians are part of one family.

"There is neither Jew nor Gentile, neither slave nor free, nor is there male and female, for you are all one in Christ Jesus." (Galatians 3:28)

"Yet to all who did receive him, to those who believed in his name, he gave the right to become children of God—children born not of natural descent, nor of human decision or a husband's will, but born of God." (John 1:12-13)

Appendix 7

Five Practices of Christians Who Are Following Jesus

1. Obey the commands of Christ

"Do not offer any part of yourself to sin as an instrument of wickedness, but rather offer yourselves to God as those who have been brought from death to life; and offer every part of yourself to him as an instrument of righteousness." (Romans 6:13)

"I am the true vine, and my Father is the gardener. He cuts off every branch in me that bears no fruit, while every branch that does bear fruit he prunes so that it will be even more fruitful. You are already clean because of the word I have spoken to you. Remain in me, as I also remain in you. No branch can bear fruit by itself; it must remain in the vine. Neither can you bear fruit unless you remain in me. I am the vine; you are the branches. If you remain in me and I in you, you will bear much fruit; apart from me you can do nothing." (John 15:1-5)

2. Pray

"Rejoice always, pray continually, give thanks in all circumstances; for this is God's will for you in Christ Jesus." (1 Thessalonians 5:16-18)

"And when you pray, do not be like the hypocrites, for they love to pray standing in the synagogues and on the street corners to be seen by others. Truly I tell you, they have received their reward in full. But when you pray, go into your room, close the door and pray to your Father, who is unseen. Then your Father, who sees what is done in secret, will reward you. And when you pray, do not keep on babbling like pagans, for they think they will be heard because of their many words. Do not be like them, for your Father knows what you need before you ask him." (Matthew 6:5-8)

3. Study the Bible

"Continue in what you have learned and have become convinced of, because you know those from whom you learned it, and how from infancy you have known the Holy Scriptures, which are able to make you wise for salvation through faith in Christ Jesus. All Scripture is God-breathed and is useful for teaching, rebuking, correcting and training in righteousness, so that the servant of God may be thoroughly equipped for every good work." (2 Timothy 3:14-17)

"Do not merely listen to the word, and so deceive yourselves. Do what it says. Anyone who listens to the word but does not do what it says is like someone who looks at his face in a mirror and, after looking at himself, goes away and immediately forgets what he looks like. But whoever looks intently into the perfect law that gives freedom, and continues in it—not forgetting what they have heard, but doing it—they will be blessed in what they do." (James 1:22-25)

4. Have fellowship with other believers

"And let us consider how we may spur one another on toward love and good deeds, not giving up meeting together, as some are in the habit of doing, but encouraging one another—and all the more as you see the Day approaching." (Hebrews 10:24-25)

5. Testify to nonbelievers

"[Jesus] said to them, 'Go into all the world and preach the gospel to all creation. Whoever believes and is baptized will be saved, but whoever does not believe will be condemned.'" (Mark 16:15-16)

"And whatever you do, whether in word or deed, do it all in the name of the Lord Jesus, giving thanks to God the Father through him." (Colossians 3:17)

Appendix 8

Global Statistics About Muslims

1900 Country	mil	1950 Country	mil	2000 Country	mil	2050 Country	mil
India	31.5	Indonesia	58.9	Indonesia	168.0	Pakistan	291.6
China	23.9	India	37.9	Pakistan`	137.1	India	230.9
Pakistan	20.9	Pakistan	35.7	India	127.6	Indonesia	207.8
Indonesia	19.4	Bangladesh	32.1	Bangladesh	110.4	Bangladesh	207.2
Bangladesh	18.8	China	21.9	Turkey	68.0	Egypt	110.8
Turkey	10.9	Turkey	21.2	Iran	65.7	Turkey	100.4
Iran	9.5	Egypt	17.5	Egypt	58.2	Nigeria	99.1
Egypt	8.5	Iran	16.6	Nigeria	48.2	Iran	96.8
Morocco	5.0	Nigeria	14.3	Algeria	29.5	Afghanistan	94.4
Afghanistan	5.0	Morocco	8.3	Morocco	29.2	Iraq	61.1
Nigeria	4.2	Afghanistan	8.0	China	25.0	Yemen	59.4
Algeria	4.0	Algeria	7.8	Iraq	24.3	Ethiopia	56.7
Sudan	3.4	Sudan	6.1	Afghanistan	23.2	Niger	48.8
Russia	3.0	Ethiopia	5.2	Sudan	21.4	Morocco	46.1
Saudi Arabia	2.7	Iraq	4.9	Ethiopia	21.2	Saudi Arabia	46.0
Yemen	2.5	Kazakhstan	4.3	Uzbekistan	20.6	Algeria	43.6
Uzbekistan	2.2	Uzbekistan	4.3	Saudi Arabia	19.9	Mali	37.0
Kazakhstan	2.1	Yemen	4.3	Yemen	17.9	Sudan	36.7
Iraq	2.0	Saudi Arabia	3.2	Syria	15.2	Uzbekistan	35.1
Ethiopia	2.0	Tunisia	3.1	Russia	14.9	China	32.9

Sub-Saharan Africa
E & SE Asia
S Asia
Arab World
C Asia
Non-Arab Middle East

Decline in order
Rise in order
New to top 20
No change

Diagram 1: The 20 countries with the largest Muslim populations

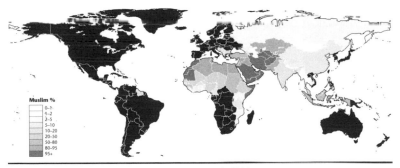

Muslim %
0–1
1–2
2–5
5–10
10–20
20–50
50–80
80–95
95+

Diagram 2: The distribution of Muslims by country in 1900

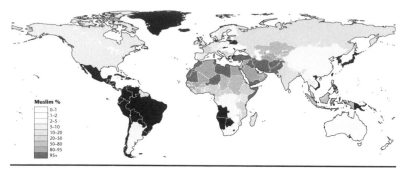

Diagram 3: The projected distribution of Muslims by country in 2050

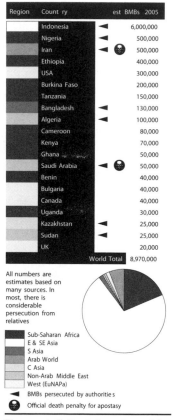

Region	Country		est BMBs 2005
	Indonesia	◄	6,000,000
	Nigeria	◄	500,000
	Iran	◄ ☠	500,000
	Ethiopia		400,000
	USA		300,000
	Burkina Faso		200,000
	Tanzania		150,000
	Bangladesh	◄	130,000
	Algeria	◄	100,000
	Cameroon		80,000
	Kenya		70,000
	Ghana		50,000
	Saudi Arabia	◄ ☠	50,000
	Benin		40,000
	Bulgaria		40,000
	Canada		40,000
	Uganda		30,000
	Kazakhstan	◄	25,000
	Sudan	◄	25,000
	UK		20,000
	World Total		8,970,000

All numbers are estimates based on many sources. In most, there is considerable persecution from relatives

Sub-Saharan Africa
E & SE Asia
S Asia
Arab World
C Asia
Non-Arab Middle East
West (EuNAPa)
◄ BMBs persecuted by authorities
☠ Official death penalty for apostasy

Diagram 4: Estimated numbers of believers from Muslim backgrounds, 2005

Charts and maps are taken from *The Future of the Global Church* by Patrick Johnstone, InterVarsity Press, 2011. Used with permission.

Notes

INTRODUCTION: THE COMMUNICATION GAP

[1]Abby Stocker, "The Craziest Statistic You'll Read About North American Missions," *Christianity Today*, August 19, 2013, www.christianitytoday.com/ct/2013/august-web-only/non-christians-who-dont-know-christians.html.
[2]"Evangelical Views of Islam," Ethics and Public Policy Center and Beliefnet (published April 7, 2003), www.beliefnet.com/News/Politics/2003/04/Evangelical-Views-Of Islam.aspx.

CHAPTER 2: COMPELLING EVANGELISM: WITNESSING LIKE JESUS

[1]David Van Biema, "Should Christians Convert Muslims?" *Time*, June 30, 2003, http://content.time.com/time/covers/0,16641,20030630,00.html.
[2]For a brief assessment of Schramm's relational communication model, see Uma Narula, *Communication Models* (New Delhi, India: Atlantic, 2006).

CHAPTER 3: COMPELLING EVANGELISM: PRACTICAL APPROACHES

[1]For more information on this specific approach, see Fouad Masri, *Adha in the Injeel* (Indianapolis: Crescent Project, 2004).

CHAPTER 11: IS THE GOSPEL OF BARNABAS TRUE?

[1]Qur'an 61:6; Saheeh International Translation (Birmingham, UK: Maktabah Booksellers and Publishers, 2010).

CHAPTER 12: USE YOUR TOOLS

[1]Based on "World Birth and Death Rates, Estimated 2011," Ecology Global Network, www.ecology.com/birth-death-rates.

crescent project

HOPE WORTH SHARING

We welcome your inquiries at:

Crescent Project
P.O. Box 50986
Indianapolis, IN 46250

www.crescentproject.org
info@crescentproject.org

Also by Fouad Masri

Adha in the Injeel

Is the Injeel Corrupted?

Ambassadors to Muslims

Bridges: Christians Connecting with Muslims
    DVD small group study